T0354167

HEARTWOOD OF THE BODHI TREE

Heartwood *of the* Bodhi Tree

The Buddha's Teaching on Voidness

Buddhadāsa Bhikkhu

Original translation from the Thai by Dhammavicayo

Edited by Santikaro Bhikkhu

Wisdom Publications
199 Elm Street
Somerville, Massachusetts 02144
wisdomexperience.org

© Evolution Liberation 1994, 2014
All rights reserved.

No part of this book may be reproduced in any form or by any means, electronic or mechan-
ical, including photocopying, recording, or by any information storage and retrieval system
or technologies now known or later developed, without permission in writing from the
publisher.

Library of Congress Cataloguing-in-Publication Information
  Phra Thepwisutthimethī (Ngü am), 1906–1993, author.
    Heartwood of the bodhi tree : the Buddha's teaching on voidness / Buddhadāsa
Bhikkhu ; original translation from the Thai by Dhammavicayo ; edited by Santikaro Bhik-
khu.
    pages cm
  Includes bibliographical references and index.
  ISBN 1-61429-152-7 (pbk. : alk. paper)
  1. Sunyata. I. Dhammavicayo, 1958– translator. II. Santikaro, Bhikkhu, 1957– editor. III.
Swearer, Donald K., 1934– writer of supplementary textual content. IV. Title.
  BQ4275.P4713 2014
  294.3'42—dc23
                    2013036979

ISBN 978-1-61429-152-7
Ebook ISBN 978-0-86171-868-9

21
7 6 5 4

Illustrations by Fan Li-Wen. Cover photo, "Gaudi Tree," by Tim Flach. Cover design
by Tony Lulek and Andy Francis. Interior design by TLLC. Set in Diacritical Garamond
11.5/15 pt.

Wisdom Publications' books are printed on acid-free paper and meet the guidelines for per-
manence and durability of the Committee on Production Guidelines for Book Longevity of
the Council on Library Resources.

Printed in the United States of America.

Contents

Foreword by Donald Swearer

> Dhamma is acting as we should act in order to be fully human throughout all the stages of our lives. Dhamma means to realize our fullest potential as individual human beings. What is most important is to realize that the Dhamma is not simply "knowing," but also "acting" in the truest sense of what it means to be human.
>
> —Buddhadāsa Bhikkhu, "The Right Action To Be Human" ("Kankratham Thi Thukdong Kae Quam Pen Manut")

THE CHALLENGING VISION OF BUDDHADĀSA BHIKKHU

AS THE ABOVE QUOTATION and the essays included in *Heartwood of the Bodhi Tree* amply demonstrate, Phra Dhammakosacarya Nguam Indapañño, better known as Buddhadāsa Bhikkhu (May 27, 1906–May 25, 1993), was one of the most creative twentieth-century thinkers in Thai Theravāda Buddhism. Only a small portion of the extensive Buddhadāsa corpus has been translated from Thai into English and other European languages, hence the importance of this volume of essays that elucidate one of major foundational themes in Buddhadāsa's thought—namely, "That nothing whatsoever should be clung to as 'I' and 'Mine.'" Or, as Buddhadāsa reiterates in one of his favorite Pali phrases, "*Sabbe dhammā nālaṁ abhinivesāya*" (Nothing whatsoever should be clung to). The concept that epitomizes non-clinging for Buddhadāsa is *suññatā*, translated in this volume as "voidness." But it is equally true for Buddhadāsa that nonclinging is the essential meaning of the Four Noble Truths, no self, interdependent co-arising, Nibbāna, and even of Buddha. The heart of Buddhism is the quenching of suffering, a condition that cannot be achieved without overcoming clinging to the self brought on by blind attachment and ignorance.

The core of Buddhadāsa's teaching might be summarized as follows: The individual is not-self. As such s/he is part of an ongoing conditioning process devoid of self-nature, a process to which words can only point. This process functions according to universal principles we call nature. It is the true, normative, and moral condition of things. To be not-self, therefore, is to be void of self, and hence to be part of the interdependent co-arising matrix of all things, and to live according to the natural moral order in a community voluntarily restrained by other-regarding concerns.

The release of this new edition of *Heartwood of the Bodhi Tree* from Wisdom Publications offers an opportunity for reflection on the challenging vision of Dhamma and its place in the world that Buddhadāsa Bhikkhu made his life's work. A dynamic, critical thinker who eschewed the Buddhist Sangha mainstream, Buddhadāsa rejected all absolutisms in a manner consistent with his foundational principle of nonclinging. He was especially critical of ideological absolutism and religious idolatry and was an advocate for environmental preservation and social justice.

The Challenge of Ideological Absolutism

Buddhadāsa's theory of two languages or two levels of language—an outer, physical, literal, conventional dimension and an inner, spiritual, symbolic dimension—challenges textual and doctrinal literalism, and simplistic, doctrinaire ideologies.

In his essay "Everyday Language / Dhamma Language" (Phasa Khon /

Phasa Tham), Buddhadāsa analyzes the meaning of many terms, some specifically religious, such as Buddha, Dhamma, *nibbāna*, and God, but ordinary words, as well; the word "person," for example. In everyday language "person" refers to the outer form, as in the sentence, "We see a person walking down the street." But in Buddhadāsa's view, to limit our understanding of "person" to the superficial, outer form ignores the profundity of the Dhamma-level meaning of the word. At the Dhamma-level "person" refers specifically to special qualities implied by the word—in particular, to the mental qualities of a lofty mind or high mindedness.

Buddhadāsa's teaching about everyday language / dhamma language resonates with similar ideas from Thích Nhât Hanh, one of the founders of socially engaged Buddhism during the Vietnam War. During that time, Nhât Hanh organized the Tiep Hien Order or Order of Interbeing. The first of the fourteen precepts of the Order of Interbeing is the following:

> Do not be idolatrous about or bound to any doctrine, theory, or ideology, even Buddhist ones. All systems of thought are only guiding means; they are not absolute truth.

To explain the precept, Nhât Hanh points to the well-known metaphor that the Buddha's teaching is a raft to cross to the farther shore of the river of samsara; the raft is not the shore, and if we cling to the raft we miss everything. In *Being Peace*, Nhât Hanh writes, "The Order of Interbeing was born in Vietnam during the war, which was a conflict between two world ideologies. In the name of ideologies and doctrines, people kill and are being killed. If you have a gun, you can shoot one, two, three, five people; but if you have an ideology and stick to it, thinking it is the absolute truth, you can kill millions." Buddhadāsa Bhikkhu and Nhât Hanh are constructive critics of ideological absolutism and scriptural literalism.

The Challenge of Religious Idolatry

Buddhadāsa also held the view that the world's great religions, while historically different, share a common ground. In his provocative Dhamma talk "No Religion!" (Mai Mi Sasana), Buddhadāsa startled his Thai Buddhist audience by saying:

> The ordinary, ignorant worldling is under the impression that there are many religions and that they are all different to the extent of being hostile and opposed. Thus one considers Christianity, Islam, and Buddhism to be incompatible and even bitter enemies. Such is the conception of the worldly person who speaks according to ordinary impressions. Precisely because of such characterizations there exist different religions hostile to one another. If, however, people penetrate to the fundamental nature of religion, they will regard all religions as essentially similar. Although they may say there is Buddhism, Christianity, Islam, and so on, they will also say that essentially they are the same. If they should go on to a deeper understanding of the Dhamma until finally they realize the absolute truth, they will discover that there is no such thing called religion—that there is no Buddhism, Christianity, or Islam. Therefore, how can they be the same or conflicting?

He expressed a similar point of view in his Sinclair Thompson lectures delivered at McGilvary Theological Seminary, Chiang Mai, Thailand, in 1967 (BE 2510):

> Christianity and Buddhism are both universal religions; they exist wherever truly religious people practice their religion in the most perfect way. If religious persons show respect for each religion's founder and for the Dhamma-truth at the core of each religion, they will understand this

interpretation. Devotion to a religion results in the cessation of self-interest and self-importance and therefore leads to a realization of the universality and unity of all religions.

Buddhadāsa's inclusive universalism is an expression of his conviction that nonattachment lies at the heart of Buddhism and all religions. Preoccupation with the external trappings of religious institutions and their ritual ceremonies represents a particular form of attachment and, consequently, obscures the true meaning of religion, which is to *transform egoism into altruism*. In the case of conventional Thai Buddhist practice, Buddhadāsa directs especially sharp criticism at the practice of merit-making rituals:

> The perception of most adherents of Buddhism is limited to what they can do to get a reward.... The heart of Buddhism is not getting things but getting rid of them. It is, in other words, nonattachment.

For Buddhadāsa, when we cling to external, outer, physical forms we see everything in dualistic terms—good or evil, merit or sin, happiness or unhappiness, gain or loss, is or is not, my religion versus their religion. Such dualistic thinking is at the heart of religious conflict. Buddhadāsa's universalism counters such a view.

THE CHALLENGE OF ENVIRONMENTAL DESTRUCTION

Buddhadāsa's concept of nature as Dhamma (*thamma pen thammachat*) challenges conventional attitudes and actions regarding the care of the earth. Buddhadāsa's perception of the liberating power of nature as Dhamma inspired him to found the Garden of Empowering Liberation (Wat Suan Mokkh) as a center for teaching and practice in Chaiya, southern Thailand. For Buddhadāsa the natural surroundings of his forest monastery were nothing less than a medium for personal transformation:

Trees, rocks, sand, even dirt and insects can speak. This doesn't mean, as some people believe, that they are spirits or gods. Rather, if we reside in nature near trees and rocks, we'll discover feelings and thoughts arising that are truly out of the ordinary. At first we'll feel a sense of peace and quiet that may eventually move beyond that feeling to a transcendence of self. The deep sense of calm that nature provides through separation from the troubles and anxieties that plague us in the day-to-day world serves to protect the heart and mind. Indeed, the lessons nature teaches us lead to a new birth beyond the suffering that comes from attachment to self. Trees and rocks, then, can talk to us. They help us understand what it means to cool down from the heat of our confusion, despair, anxiety, and suffering.

For Buddhadāsa, it is only by being in nature that the trees, rocks, earth, sand, animals, birds, and insects can teach us the lesson of forgetting the self—being at one with the Dhamma. The destruction of nature, then, implies the destruction of the Dhamma. The destruction of the Dhamma is the destruction of our humanity.

THE CHALLENGE OF SOCIAL JUSTICE

Time and again in his writings Buddhadāsa challenges conventional, literal, narrow understandings of Buddhism and all religions in favor of universal principles of human development. Buddhadāsa challenges us to go beyond simply identifying ourselves as Thai Buddhists, American Christians, or Iranian Muslims, to identify ourselves as human beings. His interpretation of the Four Noble Truths as nature, the laws of nature, the duty of humankind to live according to the laws of nature, and the consequences of following the laws of nature reflects his view that all human beings share a common natural environment, and are part of communities imbedded in the natural order of things. This interconnected universe we inhabit is the natural condition of things. To act contrary to this law of nature is to suffer, because such actions contradict reality. Consequently, the good of the individual parts is predicated on the good of the whole, and vice versa.

The ethical principle of the good of the whole is based on the truth of interdependent co-arising. Nothing exists in isolation; everything co-exists interdependently as part of a larger whole whether human, social, cosmic, or molecular:

> The entire universe is a Dhammic community (*dhammika sanghkhom*). Countless numbers of stars in the sky exist together in a Dhammic community. Because they follow the principles of a Dhammic community they survive. Our small universe with its sun and planets including the earth is a Dhammic community.

Buddhadāsa's view of a Dhammic community reflects his persistent emphasis on overcoming attachment to self, to "me-and-mine" (*tua ku khong ku*). Fundamentally, both personal and social well-being result from transforming self-attachment and self-love into empathy toward others and sympathetic action on their behalf. A Dhammic community, then, is a community based on the fundamental equality of all beings that both affirms and transcends all distinctions, be they gender, ethnicity, or class. Such a view does not deny the existence of differences among individuals or groups. But all people, regardless of position and status, should understand that their own personal well-being depends on the well-being of all.

The themes that I have highlighted in this foreword point to, but in no way exhaust, the breadth and originality of Buddhadāsa Bhikkhu's interpretation of the Buddha-Dhamma. *Heartwood of the Bodhi Tree* is a superb introduction not only to one of the key aspects of Buddhist philosophy but to one of the most original Theravāda thinkers of the modern era.

Foreword by Jack Kornfield

IN ALL OF CONTEMPORARY BUDDHISM, a handful of figures stand out for their remarkable and uncompromising teachings, their clear transmission of the timeless heart of the Buddha. There is no Theravāda master of our time whom it gives me greater pleasure to see more widely available and read than Buddhadāsa Bhikkhu. Had he lived in Japan, he would have been declared a living national treasure, and, indeed, at the end of his life he was among the best known and most respected of the masters that Thai Buddhism has produced in many centuries.

Ajahn Buddhadāsa was not interested in the ceremonial practices of Buddhism nor the common religious forms and conventions that make up most of Buddhist life in Asia. He was interested in one thing and one thing alone—the truth, at any cost. When one visited him, he received his guest as a true spiritual friend. Unlike traditional Buddhist masters, he did not want visitors to bow to him but invited them to sit next to him, speaking with great depth and heartfelt sincerity about spiritual life, questioning together as with a close friend.

His forthrightness and teaching are renowned throughout Thailand. He did not mince words. He described the busloads of visitors who stop at his monastery as its fame has grown. Decrying many who walk around as if visiting an amusement park, he said, "sometimes I think many of these people just stop here because they have to visit the bathroom." Yet when visitors were sincere, Ajahn Buddhadāsa did everything possible to translate the Dhamma, the laws of life, in the most direct and immediate fashion. He called good Dhamma teachings a "great public health measure" and deeply believed that the sublime Dhamma can be taught for all: from grandfathers and grandmothers to the youngest of students. He believed that all who wish to do so can understand the end of sorrow and awaken the great happiness of the Buddha. Even if you cannot understand non-self, he said, perhaps you can understand non-selfishness. In this simple concept, he said, the freedom and happiness of the Buddha is also to be found.

From the beginning, in the monastery that he founded just over sixty years ago, Ajahn Buddhadāsa's actions have exemplified his courageous commitment to truth. He forbade all statues of the Buddha and all the popular forms of worship and merit-making. Instead of building a large temple for the monks to meet for ceremonies, he placed great stones in a circle under the trees to create a holy place as it was in the forests of India over 2,500 years ago. He created a Dhamma hall as a theater that shows even the most uneducated villager, through pictures and words, the essence of the true teachings of the Dhamma.

When one enters his monastery, called the "Garden of Liberation," it is like finding a Zen garden surrounded by a great and ancient forest. This still and beautiful forest was chosen by Ajahn Buddhadāsa years ago because it evokes both peace and joy. Just as the Buddha invited his followers to enjoy "the happiness of life in the forest, the happiness of the life of Dhamma," all who enter the Garden of Liberation are invited to receive a quenching drink for their spirit.

In his eighties, Ajahn Buddhadāsa sat outside his cottage on a bench under the trees with restful and joyful ease. He took tremendous delight in the Dhamma, in speaking the Dhamma, in walking the Dhamma, in breathing the Dhamma. Visiting him recently after many years' absence, I found his mind as clear as ever, as light as a cloud, as open as the sky.

Ajahn Buddhadāsa spoke of the healing power of the trees and walkways of Suan Mokkh. When I asked him how so many Westerners who begin spiritual life with deep inner wounds, pain, and self-hatred can best approach practice, he replied simply with two suggestions. First, their whole spiritual practice should be enveloped by the principles of *mettā* (loving kindness). Then they should be taken out into nature, into beautiful forests or mountains. They must stay there long enough to realize that they too are a part of nature. They must rest there until they too can feel harmony with all life and their proper place in the midst of all things.

In the center of Suan Mokkh there is a lotus pond and, nearby, a Dhamma teaching hall designed in the shape of a huge boat to carry us across the stream of sorrows to the freedom of awakening. With a natural simplicity, Ajahn Buddhadāsa offers us the boat of the Dhamma, teaching the laws of life. In this book, he calls it "a handful of leaves," and, as the Buddha did, he offers us this handful of leaves as the essence of the teachings. All that we need in order to understand sorrow and freedom, to understand the whole nature of our lives, is in this handful of leaves. In these teachings he does not emphasize Theravāda, nor Mahāyāna, nor Vajrayāna, but the core or heart that transcends all Buddhist schools. The essence of Dhamma that he teaches, Ajahn Buddhadāsa calls Buddhayāna, the great vehicle of the Buddha.

This remarkable book, *Heartwood of the Bodhi Tree*, is an example of this essence. He teaches us beautifully, profoundly, and simply the meaning of *suññatā* or voidness, which is a thread that links every great school of Buddhism. He shows how a teaching that becomes central to Mahāyāna and Vajrayāna is also profoundly expressed in the earliest words of the Buddha. He teaches us the truth of this voidness with the same directness and simplicity with which he invites us into his forest. To understand voidness, he says, is to understand all dhammas, to understand voidness is to see what brings ease and peace, to understand voidness is to know that all is well.

In teaching, Ajahn Buddhadāsa used a precision and care with language, inviting us to discover deeper and deeper meanings for voidness.

In this book, Ajahn Buddhadāsa bids us to investigate and consider the nature of voidness in life. Notice the simple and remarkable things he says. He reminds us that through voidness, *nibbāna*, complete liberation, can be experienced by people in their daily life. He shows that voidness is a deep, yet common, experience for us and that whenever we experience voidness, there we find freedom. He speaks of how the Dhamma of voidness is beyond all good and bad, gain and loss, not to be cultivated or grasped, nor found through special practices and states. Instead, he shows how these most profound teachings of the Buddha are to be found within our own intimate and immediate experience.

Ajahn Buddhadāsa invites us to inquire into our true nature, to go beyond the duality of self and other, and to discover that which leads to the selfless and the deathless. In this, he teaches that voidness is the truth that underlies all things, irrespective of purity and defilement. He reminds us that the Buddha breathed with voidness and that supreme voidness is the dwelling place of all great persons. Then he brings his teaching back to earth, admonishing us each individually to realize *nibbāna* here and now.

Ajahn Buddhadāsa's teaching is based on an exquisitely careful scholarship. He has systematically extracted from all the volumes of the Buddha's words, the very heart, the essence, the pith of the Dhamma. His scholarship challenges many contemporary interpretations and throws out, as later misunderstandings, teachings of past and future lives and the whole complicated study of the Abhidhamma. He demonstrates that all of the Buddha's teachings can be directly experienced by us in each moment. When asked how we can know what is the true Buddha word, he says "the true Buddha word always speaks of voidness, rings of voidness, and anything that does not ring of voidness is not the word of the Buddha."

Ajahn Buddhadāsa's clarity and his teachings on the heart of the Buddha's awakening have inspired many of the best teachers of this generation. My first teacher, Ajahn Chah, and Ajahn Buddhadāsa would often exchange affectionate gifts back and forth when monks would travel between their forest monasteries. This book and the teachings within it are Ajahn Buddhadāsa's affectionate gift to you. It is a great and compassionate treasure that he offers. If you read and understand the deep meaning of voidness in yourself, you will discover the freedom of the deathless. And then, as the Buddha himself stated, by living rightly we ensure that the earth will not be without enlightened beings.

Preface

THE WORD *suññatā* has had a checkered history of interpretation and explanation since the Buddha's time. Now that Buddhist books abound in English, and differing teachings and interpretations are offered as Buddhist, we need to bring the teaching of *suññatā* into its proper place at the center of Buddhist study and practice. This can only be done if we correctly understand the meaning and importance of *suññatā*. We hope that this little book will help. Here, we will explore it as it appears in the Pali texts of Theravāda Buddhism.

In the southern Thailand where Buddhadāsa Bhikkhu grew up during the early 1900s, Buddhism was inseparable from the culture. That traditional, peasant Buddhism provided the belief system that underlay conscious life, the moral structure that guided social relationships, and the answers to life's difficult questions. The coming of rubber plantations, market economics, foreign experts, tourism, and modernism changed all that. The resulting capitalization and urbanization has all but destroyed the old social fabric and the moral belief system on which it was based. The old beliefs are not compatible with what is taught in the schools, on TV, and in government policies. Thai Buddhism has struggled ever since to remain true to its deepest spiritual roots and yet prove itself relevant to these modern realities. Even now, not enough people realize, as Ajahn Buddhadāsa did years ago, that only the timeless

Dhamma of *suññatā* (and sister principles) can stand up to science and guide humanity in an era of great material and technological progress.

When Buddhadāsa Bhikkhu was a young monk (in the 1930s) senior monks discouraged sermons on principles and teachings such as not-self, dependent origination, thusness, and voidness (*anattā, paṭicca-samuppāda, tathatā,* and *suññatā*). Supposedly, these were too difficult for ordinary people to understand. For the masses, moral teachings based on ancient—and not particularly Buddhist—beliefs about *karma,* rebirth, merit, heaven, and hell were considered appropriate and sufficient. Thus, the most profound teachings of the Buddha were left out of public discourse, and few monks gave them much attention, although these words regularly cropped up in their chants and studies. Only a few free thinkers and curious young monks gave these terms much attention.

In his first year as a monk, Buddhadāsa Bhikkhu spoke in his sermons of *suññatā,* because it was mentioned in his studies, but he did not fully grasp its significance. At that time, *suññatā* was generally explained as "vacancy, disappeared, nothingness," and there were many superstitious beliefs associated with it. Only after coming across the Buddha's many references to, and clear explanations of, voidness did Buddhadāsa Bhikkhu begin to understand its meaning and importance. He began to refer to it in talks more and more, even though senior monks had asked him to refrain from speaking about *anattā, suññatā,* and other "too profound Dhammas."

In a 1991 conversation, Ajahn Buddhadāsa was asked why he found it necessary to go against the wishes of senior monks and teach *suññatā.* He replied, "Because this is the heart or nucleus of Buddhism: voidness of self (*attā*). It's the essence, the quintessence of Buddhism, because most other teachings speak of *attā.* Buddhism teaches that there's nothing that ought to be regarded as being *attā.*"

When asked whether anyone knew about *suññatā,* he answered, "We aren't certain about that; terms have been used incorrectly. *Suññatā* was often translated into Thai as *suñ plao* (zeroness, vacancy, nothingness). Ordinary people and Abhidhamma fans liked to translate it as 'empty-zero,' as valueless or worthless. It was improperly translated because it was incorrectly understood. And because it was misunderstood, nobody gained any benefit from it. The Dhamma of this word had been lost. It ought to be understood simply as void of self, void from self."

In this book, Buddhadāsa Bhikkhu points out that the "heartwood," the pith, the essence of the Buddhist teachings is the practice of non-clinging. It is living with a mind void of the feelings of "I" and "mine." He masterfully shows us how to develop this practice and how to take voidness as our fundamental principle. When we do this, we have a wonderful tool for understanding and making use of every one of the many concepts and skillful means that lie within the Buddhist tradition. This tool also allows us to distinguish those things that are alien to Buddhism. Drawing fluently from material in the Pali Canon, Ajahn Buddhadāsa makes immediate and practical terms and concepts that often seem dauntingly abstract.

The text translated here represents the first time he took *suññatā* as the exclusive theme of a talk and spoke about it in great detail. At first, there was no controversy. Later, he began to explain *suññatā* in terms he thought anyone could understand; he began to speak of *cit wāng*, "void mind" (or "free mind"). Many traditionalists, scholars, and advocates of Western-style development took exception. As had happened before, Buddhadāsa Bhikkhu was criticized in the newspapers and reviled from pulpits. "This is Mahāyāna, this isn't Buddhism." In the end, *suññatā* and *cit wāng* became well-known and, in many cases, correctly understood for the first time.

Buddhadāsa Bhikkhu has been branded a heretic, Mahāyānist, communist, and more. With these intended insults he smiles, confident that he is simply living up to his name—"Slave of the Buddha"—by carrying on the Buddha's work. He knows that dogmatism and narrow-mindedness cause *dukkha*, while *suññatā* frees beings from *dukkha*. The rigidly orthodox, thus, suffer themselves. Only those who are more practical and truly open-minded can serve the Buddha by teaching the Dhamma that quenches *dukkha*. Since his first unorthodox and controversial lectures in Bangkok during the 1940s, he has taught Buddha-Dhamma as he saw and experienced it, not as later traditions dictate. Instead, he has striven to remain faithful to the tradition of the Buddha's original teaching. Unconcerned with narrow-minded sniping between Theravāda and Mahāyāna, Buddhadāsa Bhikkhu seeks, rather, Buddhayāna, the Buddha's vehicle, the original pristine Dhamma at the heart of all genuine and living Buddhist schools.

Buddhadāsa Bhikkhu's method has been to search the Pali *suttas* (discourses of the Buddha) for the Buddha's word. The task is not easy, for the scriptures are vast and the teachings many. Some of their contents seem out of place, or of temporary, limited value. Others fit together in a unified vision and practical understanding of human life that is timeless. This unitary Buddhism, which appears to be of the earliest date, can be uncovered through careful reflection and practice using certain key teachings as one's guide. This book is about the most essential teaching of all, one which, when realized, will illuminate all teachings.

The book began as three Dhamma talks given in Thai by Buddhadāsa Bhikkhu to the Buddha-Dhamma Study Club of Siriraj Hospital in Bangkok. The dates of the talks were December 17, 1961, January 7, 1962, and January 21, 1962. Later in 1962, they were transcribed and printed under the title *Kaen Buddhasat* (Heartwood of Buddha's Teaching). This book has been reprinted many times since. In 1965, it was recognized by UNESCO as an outstanding book.

Kaen Buddhasat was translated into English in 1984 by an English monk who uses the pen name "Dhammavicayo." This translation was then published by the Suan Usom Foundation in 1985 in honor of Ajahn Buddhadāsa's seventy-ninth birthday (or "age teasing," as he has preferred to call his birthdays).

This edition has been prepared with the permission and help of the original translator. The editor and various readers have made a number of small revisions, including some reorganization. In this process, the editor has consulted with Ajahn Buddhadāsa to better ensure the correct translation of his understanding of Dhamma.

A fresh look at the technical terms in this book has led to the inclusion of a number of Pali words in the text. We hope those readers who find this somewhat irritating or daunting will have the patience to stay with the argument and benefit from the points being made. In the past, it seems that a desire to make Buddhist works accessible to even the most general reader has led to unfortunate misunderstandings of even basic principles. Words like *dhamma* and *dukkha* have such a wealth of meanings and associations that no single English rendering could hope to do them justice.

We have included a glossary to help readers assimilate the Pali terms and more clearly understand Ajahn Buddhadāsa's use of them. He has given a great deal of attention to the proper definition and practical explanation of Pali terms, and he often uses them with a new twist or insight. We hope that the glossary will help the reader to better appreciate his careful use of language.

Notes have been placed at the end of the book. We hope this supplemental information will aid the reader's understanding of the text. In these notes, we have tried to give references to the Pali Canon where possible, following the designations of the Thai Tipitika. Unfortunately, we can refer to the Pali Text Society editions in some cases only, due to an incomplete reference library.

Finally, the editor would like to thank the friends who have helped with this new edition. First, to Dhammavicayo Bhikkhu, the original translator, for his help and support. Second, to Samanera Naṭṭhakaro for typing the manuscript and improving the editor's grammar and punctuation. Then, very special thanks and *anumondanā* to Dorothea Bowen for her judicious and sensitive editing. Lastly, to Ven. Losang Samden, Nick Ribush, Kate Wheeler, and the other friends at Wisdom who have made this project a reality, more or less. And, of course, to Ajahn Buddhadāsa himself for the guidance of his teaching, the example of his life, and his patience in answering endless questions. Any errors are the responsibility of the editor, who begs the forgiveness of author, translator, and reader.

Santikaro Bhikkhu
Suan Mokkhabalārāma

Editor's Note on the Meaning and Translation of Suññatā

W E HAVE YET TO FIND an English word that properly conveys the meaning of *suññatā* as the Buddha used it (according to the Pali teachings). First of all, we must avoid any misunderstanding that equates *suññatā* with nothingness, nonexistence, vacancy, vacuum, zeroness, and the like. *Suññatā* is not to be understood materially. Nor is it some kind of nihilism. Too many people have been frightened away from this teaching, and others, by such misinterpretations.

Because of the difficulty involved with translating *suññatā*, and Pali in general, Ajahn Buddhadāsa prefers that we leave it untranslated. He asks that students of Dhamma become familiar with the use and ramifications of the original Pali term. Then, if necessary, each reader may translate *suññatā* in the way that works for her: voidness, emptiness, or whatever.

Ajahn Buddhadāsa says, "If one must translate *suññatā*, 'voidness' is the best choice. 'Emptiness' is too close to 'nothingness' (*natthita-diṭṭhi*), which means 'totally empty of everything.' *Suññatā* doesn't mean 'nothing' or 'nothingness'; it means 'void of *attā*' (self). In Pali they are different terms: *suññatā* and *natthita*. They should not be confused.

If *suññatā* means 'nothingness,' then it's useless and has no benefit. It wouldn't be Dhamma."

Voidness, on the other hand, is a particular absence. It can't be void of everything. We take voidness to be conditional or referential, that is, we must stipulate void of *what*. "Emptiness" seems to lack everything, to be an utter nothingness, whereas voidness is void only of the object we specify. In the Buddha's case, it is void of self. (However, if you think "emptiness" is correct, that's OK. This is a matter of semantics. Ultimately, nobody can decide.)

In Ajahn Buddhadāsa's words, "*Suññatā* simply means 'void of self.' Anything, everything exists according to its conditions. There are *khandhas* (aggregates, heaps), there are *āyatana* (senses), but they are *anattā*, they are *suññatā*. So we feel 'void' is closer to *suñña*, which is void only of *attā*." "Void" is also used this way in the Bible: "In the beginning God created the heavens and the earth. And the earth was without form, and void..." (Gen. 1:1–2).

Ajahn Buddhadāsa tells us, "The Buddha insisted that the world is void of *attā* and void of *attaniya*, but he didn't mean it is void of other unmentioned things. Whatever word you use to translate *suññatā*, it must mean only void of self (*attā*) and void of relation to self (*attaniya*). The Buddha said that the world is *suñño* (void) but there's still a world. The world is void but it still exists; it's void of *attā*. Use whatever word you like, as long as you see the world as *suññatā*.

"It's like a material vacuum: there's nothing in it, but there's still space. It's void of air, but it still has a certain kind of space. A vacuum isn't the sort of emptiness that lacks everything. There's a certain kind of *ākāsa* (space). You can't say there's nothing."

A look at the Thai language can help us here. *Suñña*, the adjective, is translated as *wāng*, which means "void, free from, devoid of." *Suññatā* is rendered *kwam-wāng*, that is, "voidness," which includes a sense of freedom, ease, peace, and openness. It signifies that all is well, that there are no problems. In the past, *suññatā* was translated as *wāng-plao*, an altogether different thing, meaning "void of being, zeroness, vacancy, disappeared, nothing." This translation has given some social critics the excuse to attack *suññatā* as being an obstacle to the country's economic and social development, which they claim depends on desire and attachment. Ajahn Buddhadāsa counters that the only way to develop a country peacefully is with wisdom, that is, voidness. Of course, people must have the real *suññatā* in mind and heart.

In addition to *suññatā*, there are many other Pali terms for which there is no exact English equivalent. Take, for example, *dukkha*. Generally, it is translated as "suffering," occasionally as "ill, pain," and the like. We feel that none of these words captures the full meaning of *dukkha*. As Ajahn Buddhadāsa points out, even *dukkha* isn't translated correctly. "Suffering" isn't correct because even *sukha* (happiness, joy) is *dukkha*. *Sukha* has the character of *dukkha*: once you've really seen it, it's ugly.

To aid in the exploration of important Pali terms we have included a glossary of Pali terms. We recommend that the reader consult it regularly so as to be familiar with the way Ajahn Buddhadāsa uses the terms.

Exploring the meanings that the Buddha gave to Pali terms is a rich path of study and reflection. May these comments and the book they introduce help open this approach for the reader. Thus we may continue the vital work of rediscovering Dhamma (*suññatā*) in our own times, lives, realities.

The Bodhi Tree

BODHI TREE" is the nickname of the species of tree under which each Buddha awakens to *suññatā*. Each Buddha has his particular Bodhi tree. The present Buddha, Gotama, realized perfect awakening under a member of the *ficus* family, which, due to its association with Buddhism, has been given the scientific name *ficus religiosa*. In India, it is now known as the pipal tree. In Thailand, this tree and its close relatives are all known as *poh* trees. Ajahn Buddhadāsa pointed out that all members of the *ficus* family lack "heartwood" or the hard inner pith found in most trees. The heartwood of the Bodhi tree is truly void.

PART I

The Heart of Buddhism

Nothing whatsoever should be clung to as "I" or "mine."

1. Fundamental Principles

LET US INVESTIGATE the fundamental principles of Dhamma, Natural Truth.[1] I would like to discuss these essential points of Buddhism in the hope that a grasp of them will help you advance in your studies and training. If you don't grasp these points, you will get confused. You will feel that there are a great number of things to be known, and that they keep increasing until there are too many to remember, understand, or practice. This confusion is the root cause of failure; it leads to discouragement and an interest increasingly more unfocused and imprecise. In the end, it's as if one is carrying a great load of knowledge around on one's back without being able to remember, understand, or make use of it.

Therefore, I would like to focus on the essential points of Buddhism (*Buddha-sāsanā*), which are necessary for a correct understanding of Dhamma. I emphasize the fact that these points are fundamental principles, because there are some kinds of knowledge that are not fundamental, and there are some kinds that are misunderstandings deviating little by little, until they are no longer Buddhism. Or, if they are still Buddhist teachings, they are offshoots that continually branch away from the trunk.

THE QUENCHING OF DUKKHA

To call something "a fundamental principle of Buddhism" is only correct if, first, it is a principle that aims at the quenching of *dukkha* (pain, misery, suffering) and, second, it has a logic that one can see for oneself without having to believe others. These are the important constituents of such a foundation.

The Buddha refused to deal with those things that don't lead to the extinction of *dukkha*. He didn't discuss them. Take the question of whether or not there is rebirth after death. What is reborn? How is it reborn? What is its "karmic inheritance"? These questions don't aim at the extinction of *dukkha*. That being so, they are not the Buddha's teaching nor are they connected with it. They don't lie within the range of Buddhism. Also, the one who asks about such matters has no choice but to believe indiscriminately any answer that's given, because the one who answers won't be able to produce any proofs and will just speak according to his own memory and feeling. The listener can't see for herself and consequently must blindly believe the other's words. Little by little the subject strays from Dhamma until it becomes something else altogether, unconnected with the extinction of *dukkha*.

Now, if we don't raise those sorts of issues, we can ask instead, "Is there *dukkha*?" and "How can *dukkha* be extinguished?" The Buddha agreed to answer these questions. The listener can recognize the truth of every word of the answers without having to believe them blindly and can see their truth more and more clearly until he understands for himself. If one understands to the extent of being able to extinguish *dukkha*, that is the ultimate understanding. With such understanding one knows that, even at this moment, there is no person living; one sees without doubt that there is no self or anything belonging to a self. There is just the feeling of "I" and "mine" arising due to our being deluded by the beguiling nature of sense experience. With ultimate understanding, one knows that, because there is no one born, there is no one who dies and is reborn. Therefore, the whole question of rebirth is quite foolish and has nothing to do with Buddhism at all.

The Buddhist teachings aim to inform us that there is no person who is a self or belongs to a self. The sense of self is only the false understanding of the ignorant mind. There exist merely the natural processes of body and mind, which function as mechanisms for processing, interpreting, and transforming sense data. If these natural processes function in the wrong way, they give rise to foolishness and delusion, so that one feels that there is a self and things that belong to self. If the natural processes function in the correct way, those feelings don't arise. There is the original mindfulness and wisdom (*sati-paññā*), the fundamental clear knowing and true seeing that there is no "I" or "mine."

This being so, it follows that in the sphere of the Buddhist teachings there is no question of rebirth or reincarnation. Rather, there are the questions, "Is there *dukkha*?" and "How can it be quenched?" Knowing the root cause of *dukkha*, one will be able to extinguish it. And that root cause of *dukkha* is the delusion, the wrong understanding, that there is "I" and "mine."

The matter of "I" and "mine," ego and selfishness, is the single essential issue of Buddhism. The sense of "I" and "mine" is the one thing that must be purged completely. And it follows that in this principle lies the knowing, understanding, and practice of all the Buddha's teachings, without exception.

A SINGLE HANDFUL

There aren't that many fundamental, or root, principles of Dhamma. The Buddha said that his teaching is "a single handful." A passage in the *Samyutta-nikāya*[2] makes this clear. While walking through the forest, the Buddha picked up a handful of fallen leaves and asked the monks who were present to decide which was the greater amount, the leaves in his hand or all the leaves in the forest. Of course, they all said that there were many more leaves in the forest, that the difference was beyond comparison. Try to imagine the truth of this scene; clearly see how huge the difference is. The Buddha then said that, similarly, those things that he had realized were a great amount, equal

5

to all the leaves in the forest. However, what was necessary to know, things that should be taught and practiced, were equal to the number of leaves in his hand.

From this it can be seen that, compared to all the myriad things in the world, the root principles to be practiced for the complete extinction of *dukkha* amount to a single handful. We must appreciate that this single handful is not a huge amount; it's not something beyond our capabilities to reach and understand. This is the first important point that we must grasp if we want to lay the foundation for a correct understanding of the Buddha's teachings.

We must understand the word "Buddhism" (*Buddha-sāsanā*) correctly. These days, what is labeled as Buddhism or the Buddha's teaching is a very nebulous thing, because it is so extensive that it has no limit or definition. In the Buddha's time, a different word was used. The word was "Dhamma," which specifically referred to the Dhamma (or teaching) that quenches *dukkha*. The Dhamma of the Buddha was called "Samana Gotama's Dhamma." The Dhamma of another sect, say that of Nigaṇṭha Nātaputta,[3] would be called "Nigaṇṭha Nātaputta's Dhamma." One who liked a particular Dhamma would try to study until he understood it, and then he would practice accordingly. The Buddha's Dhamma was genuine and pure Dhamma, without trappings, without any of the numerous things that have come to be associated with it in later times. Now we call those trappings "Buddhism." Due to our carelessness, Buddhism has become so nebulous that it now includes many things that were originally foreign to it.

You should observe that there is Buddhism, and then there are the things associated with Buddhism. These latter things are endless in number and variety, yet we mix them up with the former and call it all "Buddhism."

The real Buddhist teachings alone are already abundant, as many as all the leaves in the forest. But what has to be studied and practiced is merely a handful. Nowadays we include those things that are merely associated with the teachings, such as the history of the religion or an explanation of the psychological aspects of the teachings. Take the *Abhidhamma* ("Higher Dhamma"): some parts of it have become psychology and some parts philosophy. It's continually expanding to fulfill the requirements of those disciplines. In addition, there are many further offshoots, so that the things associated with Buddhism have become exceedingly numerous. They have all been swept in together under the single term "Buddhism," so that it has become an enormous subject.

If we don't know how to take hold of the essential points, we will think there are too many and we won't be able to choose between them. It will be like going into a shop that sells a great variety of goods and being at a loss as to what to buy. So we just follow our common sense—a bit of this, a bit of that, as we see fit. Mostly we take those things that agree with our defilements (*kilesa*), rather than let ourselves be guided by mindfulness and wisdom. Then spiritual life becomes a matter of superstition, of rites and rituals, and of making merit by rote or to insure against some kind of fear; and there is no contact with real Buddhism.

Let us know how to separate true Buddhism from those things that have merely come to be associated with it and included under the same name. Even in the teachings themselves, we must know how to distinguish the root principles, the essential points.

2. The Spiritual Doctor

I**N THE COMMENTARIES,**[4] the Buddha is called "the spiritual doctor" because he cures "the illness of the spirit." Following some of the Buddha's teachings and their subsequent explanations in the Commentaries, there arose a distinction between two kinds of disease: physical disease and mental disease. In these texts, the term "mental disease" does not have the same meaning that it has today. In the time of the Buddha, "mental disease" referred to an illness of view (understanding, *diṭṭhi*), or defilement and craving. These days, however, it refers to ordinary mental ailments that have their base in the body and are mixed up with physical disease. To prevent differences in terminology from hindering our understanding, I would like to introduce "spiritual illness" as a third term. Let us consider physical and mental diseases as both being physical, and use the term "spiritual disease" as an equivalent of the term "mental disease" as it was used in the Buddha's time.

SPIRITUAL DISEASE

The words "spiritual" and "mental" have very different meanings. "Mental" refers to the mental factors connected to and associated with the body. If we suffer from mental illnesses, we go to a psychiatric hospital or an asylum; it's not a spiritual matter. The word "spirit" here doesn't mean anything like a ghost or a being that takes possession of people; it refers to the subtle aspects of the mind that is ill through the power of defilement, in particular through ignorance or wrong view. The mind composed of ignorance or wrong view suffers from the spiritual disease; it sees falsely. Seeing falsely causes it to think falsely, speak falsely, and act falsely. Consequently, the disease lies right there in the false thought, false speech, and false action.

You will see immediately that everyone, without exception, has the spiritual disease. As for physical and mental diseases, they only occur in some people some of the time. They are not so terrible. They don't give people the constant suffering with every inhalation and exhalation that spiritual disease does. Thus, physical and mental diseases are not dealt with in Buddhism. The Buddha's teachings are the cure for the spiritual disease and the Buddha is the spiritual doctor.

Remembering that the commentators called the Buddha "the spiritual doctor" will make it easier for us to understand each other, for everyone suffers from the spiritual disease and everyone has to cure it spiritually. That cure is Dhamma, the single handful of the Buddha's teachings that must be realized, used, and digested so as to overcome the disease.

You must pay further attention to the point that, these days, humanity pays no heed to spiritual disease, and so things are getting worse both for the individual and for society. When everyone has the spiritual disease, the whole world has it. It's a diseased world, both mentally and spiritually. Rather than lasting peace, we have permanent crisis. Moreover, as we strive and struggle, we can't find peace for even a moment. It's a waste of breath to talk about lasting peace while every side has the spiritual disease, so it's all just a matter of creating *dukkha* for oneself and one's side, as well as for the other side. It's as if a *dukkha*-making machine has appeared in the world. How then can the world find peace?

The solution lies in ending the spiritual disease within the hearts of all the world's people. What can cure it? There must be an antidote for this disease. The cure is the one handful of Dhamma.

10

This, then, is the answer to the question of why, today, the teachings are not as much of a refuge for people as Buddhism intends. It's true that many people believe that Buddhism is developing and spreading much more than previously, and that those who have a correct intellectual understanding of it are more numerous than before. And it's true that there is much study of the teachings and a greater understanding of them. However, if we don't realize that we have the spiritual disease, how will we take the teachings and make use of them? If we don't realize that we are ill, we won't go to see the doctor, and we won't take any medicine. For the most part, people don't see their illness, and merely develop a fad for collecting medicine. Although Dhamma is an effective medicine that needs to be taken internally, we merely listen to it and study it externally as an intellectual endeavor, without feeling that we are ill and in need of the medicine. We unmindfully accept the medicine in order to store it away and clutter up the place. In some cases, we use it merely as a subject for discussion or as the basis for argument and dispute. This is why Dhamma is not yet a fully effective means to cure the world.

If we are going to study Dhamma and establish Buddhist groups, we should know the ultimate aim, so that the work can proceed decisively. We should direct our effort so that Dhamma can help to treat spiritual diseases directly and quickly. Don't leave the aim so undefined that you don't know in which direction to go. Let there be just one handful of "sacred nectar" used correctly and used decisively. Then our Buddhist practice will be truly beneficial and above ridicule.

"I" AND "MINE"

Now we will explain what spiritual disease is and how a single handful of Dhamma can cure it. Spiritual disease is the disease whose germ lies in the feeling of "we" and "ours," of "I" and "mine" that is regularly present in the mind. The germ that is already in the mind develops first into the feeling of "I" and "mine" and then, acting through the influence of self-centeredness, becomes greed, hatred, and delusion, causing trouble

11

for both oneself and others. These are the symptoms of the spiritual disease that lies within us. To remember it easily, you can call it the disease of "I" and "mine."

Every one of us has the disease of "I" and "mine." We absorb more germs every time we see a form, hear a sound, smell an odor, touch a tangible object, taste a flavor, or think in the manner of an ignorant person. In other words, when the things that surround us—visual forms, sounds, odors, flavors, tangibles, and ideas—interact with their respective sense organs under the influence of ignorance, that is, without true understanding, the sense objects become germs that infect us and cause disease every time there is sense contact (*phassa*).

We must recognize this germ, which is clinging (*upādāna*), and see that it is of two kinds: attachment to "I" and attachment to "mine." Attachment to "I" is the feeling that "I" is a special entity, that I am like this or like that, that I am the greatest, or something of the sort. "Mine" is taking something as belonging to me, that which I love, that which I like. Even that which we hate is regarded as "my enemy." All this is called "mine."

In the Pali language,[5] "I" is *attā* and "mine" is *attanīyā*. As an alternative, we may use the terms generally used in Indian philosophy. The word *ahaṁkāra*, "I-ing," means having or making the feeling of "I," and it stems from the word *ahaṁ*, "I." The word *mamaṁkāra* means "my-ing," having or making the feeling of "mine," and it stems from the word *mama*, "mine."

The feelings of I-ing and my-ing are so dangerous and poisonous that we call them the "spiritual disease." Every branch of philosophy and Dhamma in the Buddha's time wanted to wipe them out. Even the followers of other creeds had the same aim of wiping out I-ing and my-ing. The difference between other creeds and Buddhism is that when they eradicated those feelings, they called what remained the "True Self," the "Pure *Atman*," the "Person." Buddhism refused to use these names because it didn't want to cause any new attachment to self or things belonging to a self. The state free of I-ing and my-ing is considered simply to be a perfect voidness. This voidness is called *nibbāna*, as in the phrase, "*Nibbāna* is the supreme voidness" (*Nibbānaṁ paramaṁ suññaṁ*). *Nibbāna* is absolutely void of "I" and void of "mine," in every possible respect, without any remainder. Such is *nibbāna*, the end of spiritual disease.

This matter of "I" or "mine" is very hard to see. If you don't take a genuine interest in it, you won't be able to understand that it is the force behind *dukkha*, the power behind spiritual disease.

Ego, Egoism, and Selfishness

That which is called *attā* or "self" corresponds to the Latin word "ego." If the feeling of self-consciousness arises, we call it egoism because once the feeling of "I" arises, it naturally and inevitably gives rise to the feeling of "mine." Therefore the feeling of self and the feeling of things belonging to self, taken together, are egoism. Ego can be said to be natural to living beings and, moreover, to be their center. If the word "ego" is translated into English, it must be rendered as "soul," a word corresponding to the Greek *kentricon*, which means "center." Thus, relating these three words, the soul (*attā*) can be regarded as the center of living beings, as their necessary nucleus. Since it is so central, ordinary people cannot easily rid themselves of the ego.

It follows that all unenlightened people must experience this feeling of egoism arising continually. Although it is true that it doesn't express itself all the time, it does manifest whenever one sees a form, hears a sound, smells an odor, touches a tactile object, or has a thought arise in the mind. On every occasion that the feeling of "I" and "mine" arises, we can take it to be the disease fully developed, regardless of whether it's dependent upon seeing a form, hearing a sound, smelling an odor, or whatever. Whenever an experience sparks the feelings of "I" and "mine," the disease is considered fully developed and the feeling of selfishness becomes more intense.

At this point, we no longer call it egoism but selfishness, because it's an agitated egoism that leads one into low, false ways, into states of thinking only of oneself without consideration for others. Everything one does is selfish. One is completely ruled by greed, hatred, and delusion. The disease expresses itself as selfishness and then harms both oneself and others. It is the greatest danger to the world. That the world is currently so troubled and in such turmoil is due to nothing other than the selfishness of each person and of all the many factions that form into competing groups. They are fighting each other without any real desire to fight, but through compulsion, because they can't control this thing. They can't withstand its force, and so the disease takes root. The world has taken in the germ, which has then caused the disease, because no one is aware of what can resist the disease, namely, the heart of Buddhism.

NOTHING WHATSOEVER SHOULD BE CLUNG TO AS "I" OR "MINE"

Let us clearly understand this phrase, "the heart of Buddhism." Whenever we ask what the heart of Buddhism is, there are so many contending replies that it's like a sea of voices. Everyone has an answer. Whether they are correct or not is another matter. It isn't good enough to answer according to what we have heard and memorized. We must each look into ourselves and see with our own mindfulness and wisdom (*sati-pañña*) whether or not we have the true heart of Buddhism.

Some will probably say the Four Noble Truths (*ariya-sacca*), others impermanence, unsatisfactoriness, and selflessness (*aniccatā, dukkhatā,* and *anattatā*), and others may cite the verse:

> Refraining from doing evil (*Sabba pāpassa akaranaṁ*),
> Doing only good (*Kusalassūpasampadā*),
> Purifying the mind (*Sacitta pariyodapanaṁ*),
> This is the Heart of Buddhism (*Etaṁ Buddhānasāsanaṁ*).[6]

All these replies are correct, but only to a degree. I would like to suggest that the heart of Buddhism is the short saying "Nothing whatsoever should be clung to." There is a passage in the *Majjhima-nikāya* where someone approached the Buddha and asked him whether he could summarize his teachings in one phrase and, if he could, what it would be. The Buddha replied that he could, and he said, "*Sabbe dhammā nālaṁ abhinivesāya.*"[7] *Sabbe dhammā* means "all things," *nālaṁ* means "should not be," *abhinivesāya* means "to be clung to."[8] Nothing whatsoever should be clung to. Then the Buddha emphasized this point by saying that whoever had heard this core phrase had heard all of Buddhism; whoever had put it into practice had practiced all of Buddhism; and whoever had received the fruits of practicing it had received all the fruits of Buddhism.

Now, if anyone realizes the truth of this point, that there is not a single thing that should be clung to, then they have no germ to cause the diseases of greed, hatred, and delusion, or of wrong actions of any kind, whether by body, speech, or mind. So whenever forms, sounds, odors, flavors, tangible objects, and mental phenomena crowd in, the antibody "Nothing whatsoever should be clung to" will resist the disease superbly. The germ will not be let in, or, if it is allowed in, it will be destroyed. The germ will not spread and cause the disease because it is continually destroyed by the antibody. There will be an absolute and perpetual immunity. This then is the heart of Buddhism, of all Dhamma. Nothing whatsoever should be clung to: *Sabbe dhammā nālaṁ abhinivesāya.*

A person who realizes this truth is like someone who has an antibody that can resist and destroy a disease. It's impossible for him or her to suffer from the spiritual disease. However, for ordinary people who don't know the heart of Buddhism, it's just the opposite. They lack even the slightest immunity.

By now you probably understand the spiritual disease and the doctor who heals it. But it's only when we see that we ourselves have the disease that we become really serious about healing ourselves, and in the right way too. Before, we didn't notice our sickness; we just enjoyed ourselves as we pleased. We were like people unaware that they have some serious illness, such as cancer or TB, who just indulge

15

in pleasure-seeking without bothering to seek any treatment until it's too late, and then die of their disease.

We won't be that foolish. We will follow the Buddha's instruction: "Don't be heedless. Be perfect in heedfulness."[9] Being heedful people, we should take a look at the way in which we are suffering from the spiritual disease and examine the germ that causes the infection. If you do this correctly and unremittingly, you will certainly receive in this life the best thing that a human being can receive.

We must look more closely into the point that clinging is the germ and then investigate how it spreads and develops into the disease. If you've observed even slightly, you will have seen that it's this clinging to "I" and "mine" that is the chief of all the defilements.

GREED, HATRED, AND DELUSION

We can divide the defilements (*kilesa*) into greed, hatred, and delusion (*lobha, dosa,* and *moha*); or group them into sixteen types; or however many categories we want. In the end, they all are included in greed, hatred, and delusion. But these three, too, can be collected into one: the feeling of "I" and "mine." The feeling of "I" and "mine" is the inner nucleus that gives birth to greed, hatred, and delusion. When it emerges as greed, blind desire, and craving, it attracts the sense object that has made contact. If, at another moment, it repels the object, that is hatred or *dosa*. On those occasions when it's stupefied and doesn't know what it wants, hovering around the object, unsure whether to attract or repel, that is delusion or *moha*.

This way of speaking makes it easier for us to observe the actual defilements. Greed or lust (*lobha* or *rāga*) pulls the object in, gathers it into itself. Hatred or anger (*dosa* or *kodha*) pushes things away. Delusion (*moha*) spins around uncertain what it should do, running in circles, afraid to push and unwilling to pull.

Defilement behaves in one of these ways toward sense objects (forms, sounds, odors, flavors, and tangible objects) depending on what form the object takes, whether it is clearly apprehensible or hidden, and whether it encourages attraction, repulsion, or confusion. Despite their differences, all three are defilements because they have their roots in the inner feeling of "I" and "mine." Therefore, it can be said that the feeling of "I" and "mine" is the chief of all defilements and the root cause of all *dukkha* and of all disease.

Having not fully appreciated or examined the Buddha's teaching regarding *dukkha*, many people have misunderstood it. They have taken it to mean that birth, old age, sickness, death, and so on are themselves *dukkha*. In fact, those are just its characteristic vehicles. The Buddha summarized his explanation of *dukkha* by saying, "In short, *dukkha* is the five aggregates (*khandha*) in which there is clinging (*upādāna*)." In Pali it's "*Sankhittena pañcupādānak-khandā-dukkhā.*" This means that anything that clings or is clung to as "I" or "mine" is *dukkha*. Anything that has no clinging to "I" or "mine" is not *dukkha*. Therefore birth, old age, sickness, death, and so on, if they are not clung to as "I" or "mine," cannot be *dukkha*. Only when birth, old age, sickness, and death are clung to as "I" or "mine" are they *dukkha*. The body and mind are the same. Don't think that *dukkha* is inherent in the body and mind. Only when there is clinging to "I" or "mine" do they become *dukkha*. With the pure and undefiled body and mind, that of the Arahant, there is no *dukkha* at all.

17

3. Voidness, or Suññatā

W E MUST SEE that the sense of "I" and "mine" is the root cause of all forms of *dukkha*. Wherever there is clinging, there is the darkness of ignorance (*avijjā*). There is no clarity because the mind is not void (*suñña*); it is shaken up, frothing and foaming with the feeling of "I" and "mine." In direct contrast, the mind that is free of clinging to "I" and "mine" is void, serene, and full of mindfulness and wisdom (*sati-paññā*).

If one speaks intelligently and concisely about voidness—although it is somewhat frightening—one speaks like a Zen master. Huang Po said that *suññatā* (voidness) is the Dhamma, *suññatā* is the Buddha, and *suññatā* is the One Mind.[10] Confusion, the absence of *suññatā*, is not the Dhamma, is not the Buddha, and is not the One Mind. It is a new concoction. There are these two diametrically opposed things that arise—voidness (*suññatā*) and confusion. Once we have understood them, we will understand all Dhamma easily.

We must firmly grasp the fact that there are two kinds of experience: on the one hand, that of "I" and "mine," and, on the other, that of mindfulness and wisdom. We also must see that the two are totally antagonistic; only one can be present at a time. If one enters the mind, the other springs out. If the mind is rife with "I" and "mine," *sati-paññā* cannot enter; if there is mindfulness and wisdom, the "I" and "mine" disappear. Freedom from "I" and "mine" is *sati-paññā*.

Right now, you who are concentrating on this teaching are void, you are not concocting the feeling of "I" and "mine." You are attending, and you have mindfulness and wisdom; the feeling of "I" and "mine" cannot enter. But if on another occasion something impinges and gives rise to the feeling of "I" and "mine," the voidness or *sati-paññā* you feel now will disappear.

If we are void of egoism, there is no experience of "I" and "mine." We have the mindfulness and wisdom that can extinguish *dukkha* and is the cure for the spiritual disease. At that moment, the disease cannot be born, and the disease that has already arisen will disappear as if picked up and thrown away. At that moment, the mind will be completely filled with Dhamma. This demonstrates that voidness is *sati-paññā*, voidness is the Dhamma, voidness is the Buddha, because in that moment of being void of "I" and "mine" there will be present every desirable quality in all of the Buddhist scriptures.

ALL VIRTUE IN VOIDNESS

To put it simply, in a moment of voidness, all the virtues are present. There is perfect mindfulness and self-awareness (*sati-sampajañña*), perfect sense of shame about doing evil (*hiri*), perfect fear of doing evil (*ottappa*), perfect patience and endurance (*khanti*), perfect gentleness (*soracca*), perfect gratitude (*kataññū-katavedī*), and perfect honesty (*sacca*). And, in voidness, there is the knowledge and vision according to reality (*yathābhūta-ñāṇadassana*) that is the cause for the fruition of the path and the attainment of *nibbāna*.

I've come down to basics, saying that there must be mindfulness and self-awareness, shame about doing evil, fear of doing evil, patience, gentleness, gratitude, and honesty—because these are also Dhamma. They too can be a refuge for the world. Even with *hiri* and *ottappa* alone, the aversion and shame toward doing evil and the fear of doing evil, the world would be tranquil with lasting peace. Nowadays there seem to be many callous people who have no sense of fear or shame with regard to doing evil. Being that way, they are able to do improper things and insist on doing them continually. Even when they see that their actions will create disaster for the whole world, they still persist, and so the world is being destroyed because it lacks even this small virtue.

Or we may take an even humbler virtue, that of gratitude (*kataññū-katavedī*). With just this one virtue, the world could be at peace. We must recognize that every person in the world is the benefactor of everyone else. Never mind people, even cats and dogs are benefactors of humanity, even sparrows are. If we are aware of our debt of gratitude to these things, we will be unable to act in any way that harms or oppresses them. With the power of this single virtue of gratitude we can help the world.

It follows that those things that take the name of virtue, if they are real virtues, have an identical nature: every one of them has the power to help the world. But if virtues are false, they become obstructive, a disordered mass of contradictions. When there is true virtue—one that is void of "I" and "mine"—all of the Dhammas and all of the Buddhas can be found in it. All things are present within the one mind that is the true mind, the mind in its true state.

On the other hand, the mind that is feverishly proliferating with "I" and "mine" is without virtue. In those moments, there is no mindfulness or self-awareness. The mind is in a rash, hasty state. There is no forethought and consideration, no restraint. There is ahiri and *anottappa*, shamelessness and no fear of doing evil. One is callous regarding evil actions, and one is without gratitude. The mind is so enveloped in darkness that one can do things that destroy the world. There's no use talking about the clear knowledge and vision of impermanence, unsatisfactoriness, and selflessness. All wholesome qualities are incomprehensible to a mind in such a lowly state.

Thus, we must be aware of these two kinds of mind: void of "I" and not void of "I." We refer to the former as "void" and the latter as "disturbed" or "busy."

A MIND UNDISTURBED

Here your common sense may say that nobody likes being disturbed. Everyone likes to be void in one way or another. Some people like the lazy voidness of not having to work. Everyone likes to be void of the annoyance of having noisy children bothering them. However, these types of voidnesses are external; they are not true voidness.

Inner voidness (*suññatā*) means to be truly normal and natural, to have a mind that is not scattered and confused. Anyone who experiences this really appreciates it. If voidness develops to its greatest degree, which is to be absolutely void of egoism, then it is *nibbāna*.

The disturbed mind is just the opposite. It is disturbed in every way—physically, mentally, and spiritually. It is totally confused, without the slightest peace or happiness. In *suññatā* is Dhamma, is Buddha, is the mind's original nature. In busyness there is no Dhamma and no Buddha, no matter how many times we shout and holler "To the Buddha I go for refuge" (*Buddhaṁ saraṇaṁ gacchāmi*).[11] It is impossible for there to be Dhamma in the busy mind. For people whose minds are disturbed by "I" and "mine"—even if they take refuge in the Triple Gem, receive the precepts, offer alms, and make merit—there can be no true Buddha, Dhamma, or Sangha present. Everything becomes just a meaningless ritual. The true Buddha, Dhamma, and Sangha abide in the void mind. Whenever the mind is void of "I" and "mine," the Triple Gem is present right there. If it is void for only a while, that is temporary Buddha, Dhamma, and Sangha. If it is absolute voidness, that is real and enduring Buddha, Dhamma, and Sangha.

Please keep making the effort to void your minds of "I" and "mine": then the Buddha, Dhamma, and Sangha will be present regularly. Keep voiding the mind until the voidness is perfect, until it is absolute. We must take Dhamma, which is simultaneously the cure of the spiritual disease and the antibody that builds immunity, and we must put it to use in our mind, so that there is no way for the disease to be born.

PART II

All About Voidness

Nothing whatsoever should be clung to as "I" or "mine."

4. All Teachings, All Practices

S uññatā (VOIDNESS) is the most difficult to understand of all the Buddhist teachings, because it is the innermost heart of Buddhism. Whatever is called the "heart" must be something subtle and profound. True understanding of it does not lie within the scope of mere conjecture or the sort of ordinary pondering to which people are accustomed. It can only be understood by determined study.

In Buddhism, the essential meaning of the word "study" is the unceasing, dedicated observation and investigation of whatever arises in the mind, be it pleasant or unpleasant.[12] Only those familiar with the observation of mind can really understand Dhamma. Those who merely read books cannot understand and, what's more, may even go astray. But those who try to observe the things going on in the mind, and always take what is true in their own minds as their standard, never get muddled. They are able to comprehend *dukkha* and ultimately will understand Dhamma. Then they will understand the books they read.

When we say that someone has a lot of spiritual experience, we mean that they are always observing the things happening in the mind. From the moment of birth to the time of death, we must train ourselves in this way. We must examine the contact of the mind with the objects that surround it and the nature of the results of that contact. Inevitably, in this natural process there will be both painful aspects and nonpainful aspects; observing them will make the mind wiser and more resilient. If we observe the direction of thoughts that generate a mind emptied of *dukkha*, this is the very best knowledge there is. Through it we gain familiarity with the experience, understanding, and realization of *suññatā*, which is a matter most profound and subtle.

We have spoken of the spiritual disease from which we all suffer, and we have described its germ as the feeling of "I" and "mine." This disease is an illness affecting mindfulness and wisdom (*sati-paññā*), that which is able to know our life and the world as they truly are. So spiritual disease refers to ignorance (*avijjā*), or the wrong understanding that springs from ignorance, and it causes the wrong actions that lead to *dukkha*, even if physically and mentally we are quite healthy.

When we are suffering from spiritual disease, with what must we treat it? We must treat it with *suññatā*. *Suññatā* is not only the cure of the disease, it is also the freedom from disease. There is nothing beyond voidness.

The medicine that cures the disease is the knowledge and practice that gives birth to *suññatā*. When voidness has appeared it will be the cure of the disease. After recovery from the disease, there will be nothing save *suññatā*, the state void of *dukkha* and void of the mental defilements that are the causes of *dukkha*. This voidness, in its broadest meaning, is void in and of itself; nothing can touch it, concoct it, improve it, or do anything to it. Thus, voidness is a reality without end or bounds, for it knows neither birth nor death. Its "being" is not the same as the being of things that are born and die; so we say that voidness has "being" characterized by immutable *suññatā*, because we have no other word to use. If anyone's mind realizes this, such realization will be the medicine that cures the disease and leads to the immediate recovery from the disease—a state timelessly void, which is true health.

THE MEANING OF *SUÑÑATĀ*

Please keep trying to grasp the meaning of this word "voidness," or *suññatā*, as we consider it from every angle.

First, consider the fact that the Buddha declared that every word that he, the Tathāgata,[13] spoke referred to the subject of *suññatā*. He spoke of no other matter, either directly or indirectly. Any talk unconnected with the subject of voidness is not the speech of the Tathāgata but of disciples of later times who liked to speak at great length to show how clever and articulate they were. As for the Tathāgata's words, they are short, spare, and straight to the point—*suññatā*. The essence of his teaching[14] is being void of *dukkha* and the defilements (*kilesa*), which are the causes of *dukkha*.

One can, if one wants, describe *suññatā* in many ways: being void of self, or void of having anything as self or as belonging to self. The word "voidness" has a whole host of applications. Although the characteristic of voidness remains constant, its expressions are innumerable. That being so, we aim to examine voidness only as absence of *dukkha* and the defilements that cause *dukkha*, and as the absence of the feeling that there is a self or that there are things that are the possessions of a self. This is voidness as it relates to our practice of Dhamma.[15]

If we ask which of the Buddha's statements concerning this matter can be taken as authoritative, we will find that in many places the Buddha taught us to know how to look on the world as being void. For example, there is the phrase, "*Suññato lokaṁ avekkhassu mogharāja sadā sato.*" Essentially, this means, "You should look on the world as being void. When you are always mindful of the *suññatā* of the world, death will not find you." The meaning also can be taken as, "When anyone sees the world as being void, they will be above the powers of *dukkha*, the chief of which is death."[16]

These words of the Buddha, enjoining us to see the world as being void, show that *suññatā* is the highest thing. Anyone who wants to be without problems concerning *dukkha* and death should look on all things, as they truly are, as being void of "I" and "mine." Two more quotes show the benefits of voidness:

27

Nibbāna is the supreme voidness
(*Nibbānaṁ paramaṁ suññaṁ*).[17]

Nibbāna is the supreme happiness
(*Nibbānaṁ paramaṁ sukham*).[18]

You must understand that *nibbāna*, the remainderless quenching of *dukkha*, has the same meaning as supreme voidness (*paramaṁ suññaṁ*). Thus, we should understand that it is possible to know and realize a voidness that is not supreme, a voidness that is in some way imperfect, incomplete, or not fully correct, that is not yet supreme voidness. For us to realize supreme voidness, we must penetrate with mindfulness and wisdom so impeccably clear that there is not the slightest feeling of "self" or "belonging to self." To say that the supreme voidness is *nibbāna*, or is identical to *nibbāna*, means that *suññatā* is the final quenching of all things that are blazing in flames. *Suññatā* is the supreme quenching of all things that are spinning and changing in streams and whirlpools. Thus, the supreme voidness and the supreme quenching are one and the same.

As for the saying that "*nibbāna* is the supreme happiness," this is an expression in the language of relative truth, a sort of enticing propaganda in the language of ordinary people, used because people are generally infatuated with happiness and want nothing else. So it is necessary to say that *nibbāna* is happiness, and what's more, that it's the best happiness. Truly speaking, *nibbāna* is better than happiness, is beyond happiness, because it is void. We shouldn't speak of it as either happiness or suffering because it lies beyond both the suffering and the happiness commonly known by us. Yet when we speak like this, people don't understand. So we must say instead, in the conventional language of the worldly, that it is ultimate happiness. This being so, when using the word happiness, we must be careful to use it properly. It is not the happiness that people generally can see or aspire to. It is a different sort of happiness, a completely new meaning of happiness: the state void of every single thing that concocts, proliferates, flows, spins, and changes.

28

Thus, it is truly lovely, truly refreshing, and truly desirable. For if there is still flux and change, constant swaying and rocking, how can there be happiness?

The feelings of sensual pleasure that arise from contact with the various sense objects are illusory; they are not ultimate happiness. Common happiness is not the supreme happiness of *nibbāna*, which is voidness. So in hearing the phrase *"Nibbāna is the supreme happiness,"* don't jump to the conclusion that *nibbāna* is exactly what you've been looking for all along and start dreaming about it without taking into consideration that it is supreme voidness.

NOTHING WHATSOEVER SHOULD BE CLUNG TO AS "I" OR "MINE"

The saying of the Buddha that deals with the practice regarding *suññatā* is the saying that is the heart of Buddhism. It requires our careful attention.

> Nothing whatsoever should be clung to as "I" or "mine"
> (*Sabbe dhammā nālaṁ abhinivesāya*).

If one amplifies the meaning a little, it may be rendered as "No one should grasp at or cling to anything as being 'I' or 'mine.'" "No one" means that there are no exceptions. "Should grasp or cling" means to give rise to ego-consciousness. "As being 'I'" refers to the feeling called "I-ing" (*ahaṁkāra*, the grasping at a soul or abiding ego-entity). "As being 'mine'" refers to the feeling called "my-ing" (*mamaṁkāra*, the grasping at phenomena as being connected to ego). So don't feel I-ing or my-ing with regard to anything at all—starting from worthless specks of dust; through valuable objects such as diamonds, sapphires, and gems; on to sexuality and sensuality; up to even higher things, namely, Dhamma in its three aspects of learning, practice, and penetration; and finally the three levels of penetration: the path realizations (*magga*), their fruits (*phala*), and *nibbāna*. Nothing whatsoever should

29

be grasped at or clung to as being "I" or "mine." This is the heart of Buddhism. The Buddha himself declared that this is the summation of all the Tathāgata's teaching.

He said that to have heard the phrase *Sabbe dhammā nālaṁ abhinivesāya* is to have heard everything; to have put it into practice is to have practiced everything; and to have reaped its fruits is to have reaped every fruit. So we need not be afraid that there is too much for us to understand. When the Buddha compared the things that he had realized, which were as many as all the leaves in the forest, with those he taught his followers to practice, which were a single handful, the single handful he referred to was just this principle of not grasping at or clinging to anything as being self or as belonging to self.

"To hear this phrase is to hear everything," because all subjects are contained within it. Of all the things the Buddha taught, there wasn't one that didn't deal with *dukkha* and the elimination of *dukkha*.[19] Grasping and clinging is the cause of *dukkha*. When there is grasping and clinging, that is *dukkha*. When there is no grasping and clinging— that is, being void of grasping and clinging—there is no *dukkha*. The practice is to make the nonarising of grasping and clinging absolute, final, and eternally void, so that no grasping and clinging can ever return. Just that is enough. There is nothing else to do.

ALL PRACTICES IN ONE

"This practice is every practice." Can you think of anything that remains to be practiced? In a given moment, if a person—whether Mr. Smith, Mrs. Jones, or anyone at all—has a mind free of grasping and clinging, at that moment, what does the person have? Please think it over. We can see that the person has attained all the traditional practices: the Triple Refuge (*tisaraṇa*), giving (*dāna*), virtuous conduct (*sīla*), meditation (*samādhi*), the discernment of truth (*paññā*), and even the path-realizations, their fruits, and *nibbāna*.

At that moment of nongrasping, one has certainly attained the first practice, that of the Triple Refuge. One has reached the Buddha, the Dhamma, and the Sangha, for to have a heart free of the mental defilements and *dukkha* is to be one with the heart of the Triple Gem (*tiratana*). One has reached them without having to chant *Buddhaṁ saraṇaṁ gacchāmi*. Crying out *Buddhaṁ saraṇaṁ gacchāmi* and so on is just a ritual, a ceremony of entrance, an external matter. It doesn't penetrate to the Buddha, Dhamma, and Sangha in the heart. If at any moment a person has a mind void of grasping at and clinging to "I" and "mine," even if only for an instant, the mind has realized voidness. The mind is clean, clear, and calm. It is one and the same as the heart of the Buddha, the Dhamma, and the Sangha. If there is a moment in which one's mind is void of "I" and "mine," in that moment, one has taken refuge and has reached the Triple Gem.

The next practice is giving (*dāna*) or making donations. The meaning of giving and sharing is to let go, to relinquish and give away, to end all grasping at and clinging to things as being "I" or "mine." As for giving in order to receive a much greater reward, such as giving a tiny amount and asking for a mansion up in heaven, that's not giving, it's just a business deal. Giving must have no strings attached. It must cast off the things that we grasp at and cling to as being "I" and "mine." At the moment that one has a mind void of ego-consciousness, then one has made the supreme offering, for when even the self has been given up, what can there be left to give? When the "I-feeling" has come to an end, the "mine-feeling" will vanish by itself. Thus, at any moment that a person has a mind truly void of self, when even the self has been completely relinquished, he or she has developed giving to its perfection.

To move on to virtuous conduct or ethics (*sīla*), one whose mind is void and free of grasping at and clinging to a self or possession of self is one whose bodily and verbal actions are truly and perfectly virtuous. Any other sort of ethics or morality is just an up-and-down affair. We may make resolutions to refrain from this and abstain from that, but we can't keep them. It's up and down because we don't know how to let go of self and the possessions of self from the start. There being no freedom from self, there can be no real morality or normalcy; or, if there is, it's inconsistent. It is not the virtuous conduct that is satisfying to the Noble Ones (*ariyakantasīla*). It is still worldly morality, continually going up and down. It can never become transcendent (*lokuttara*) morality. Whenever the mind is void, even if it's only for a moment, or a day, or a night, one has true *sīla* for all of that time.

As for concentration or collectedness (*samādhi*), the void mind has supreme *samādhi*, the superbly focused firmness of mind. A strained and uneven sort of concentration isn't the real thing. Further, any kind of *samādhi* that aims at anything other than nonclinging to the five aggregates (*khanda*) is wrong or perverted *samādhi* (*micchā-samādhi*). You should be aware that there is both wrong *samādhi* and right *samādhi*. Only the mind that is void of grasping at and clinging to "I" and "mine" can have the true and perfect stability of correct concentration (*sammā-samādhi*). One who has a void mind always has correct *samādhi*.

The next practice is *paññā* (intuitive wisdom, the discernment of truth). Here we can see most clearly that knowing *suññatā*, realizing voidness—or being voidness itself—is the essence of wisdom. At the moment that the mind is void, it is supremely keen and discerning. In contrast, when delusion and ignorance envelop and enter the mind, causing grasping at and clinging to things as self or possessions of self, then there is supreme foolishness. If you think it over, you will easily and clearly see for yourself that when delusion and ignorance have left the mind, there can be no foolishness. When the mind is void of foolishness, void of "I" and "mine," there is perfect knowing or *paññā*. So the wise say that *suññatā* and *paññā* (or *sati-paññā*, mindfulness and wisdom) are one. It's not that they are two similar things; they are one and the same thing. True or perfect *paññā* is voidness, absence of the delusion that foolishly clings. Once the mind is rid of delusion, it discovers its primal state, the true original mind, which is *paññā* or *sati-paññā*.

The word "mind" (*citta*) is being used here in a specific way. Don't confuse it with the 89 *cittas* or the 121 *cittas* of the *Abhidhamma*, which are a different matter. That which we call the original mind, the mind that is one with *paññā*, refers to the mind void of grasping at and clinging to self. Actually, this state shouldn't be called mind at all, it should be called *suññatā*, but since it has the property of knowing we call it mind. Different schools can call it what they want, but, strictly speaking, it's enough to say that the true fundamental nature of mind is *sati-paññā*, freedom from grasping and clinging. In voidness lies perfect wisdom.

We can go on to the path-realizations, their fruits, and *nibbāna*. Here the progressively higher levels of voidness reach their culmination in *nibbāna*, which is called supreme voidness (*paramasuññatā* or *paramaṁ suññaṁ*). When practice culminates in a level of insight that cuts through the fetters (*saṁyojana*) on one level or another, it is called *magga* (path-realization). The fruit (*phala*) of cutting through those fetters is the experience of liberation, either partial or complete, depending on the level of insight. With each *magga-phala* there is a corresponding realization of the unconditioned coolness (*nibbāna*), which may be a temporary glimpse or the final emancipation.

Now you may see that from taking refuge and progressing through giving (*dāna*), virtuous conduct (*sīla*), concentration (*samādhi*), and wisdom (*paññā*) there is nothing other than *suññatā*, or nonclinging to self. Even in the path-realizations, their fruits, and *nibbāna*, there's nothing more than voidness. In fact, they are its highest, most supreme level.

Consequently, the Buddha declared that to have heard this teaching is to have heard all teachings, to have put it into practice is to have done all practices, and to have reaped the fruits of that practice is to have reaped all fruits: Nothing whatsoever should be clung to as "I" or "mine" (*Sabbe dhammā nālaṁ abhinivesāya*). You must strive to grasp the essence of what this word "voidness" really means.

5. Not Clinging to Any Thing

NOW LET US CONSIDER that all things are included in
the term *dhamma*,[20] which means "thing"; *sabbe dhammā*
means "all things." When you use the term "all things," you
must be clear as to what it signifies. "All things" must refer to absolutely
everything without any exceptions. Whether something is worldly or
spiritual, material, or mental, it will always be included in "all things."
Even if there were something outside of these categories, it would
still be included in "all things" and would be contained in *dhamma*.
I would like you all to observe that worlds of material things, namely,
all realms of material objects, are *dhammas*. The mind that knows all
worlds is a *dhamma*. If the mind and the world come into contact, that
contact is a *dhamma*. If any result of that contact arises, it is a *dhamma*,
whether it's an emotion of love, hate, dislike, or fear, or whether it's
sati-paññā, the clear seeing of things as they truly are. Right or wrong,
good or bad, they are all *dhammas*. If *sati-paññā* gives rise to a succes-
sion of knowledges, those knowledges are *dhammas*. If those knowledges lead to the practice of morality, concentration, and wisdom,
or any other type of practice, that practice is a *dhamma*. The natural
results of right practice, known as the path-realizations, their fruits,
and *nibbāna*, are *dhammas* also.

In short, they are all *dhammas*. The word *dhamma* encompasses everything from the truly peripheral and superficial, the world of material objects, up to the results of Dhamma practice, the path, fruits, and *nibbāna*. Seeing each of these things clearly is called seeing "all things." And the Buddha taught that none of these things whatsoever should be grasped at or clung to as "I" or "mine."

This body cannot be grasped at or clung to. Even more so the mind: it is an even greater illusion than matter is. Thus, the Buddha said that if one is determined to cling to something as self, it would be better to cling to the body because it changes more slowly.[21] It is not as deceptive as the mind, which is immaterial and intangible (*nāmadhamma*). Mind here does not refer to the mind previously spoken of as being one and the same thing as voidness, but to the mentality and assorted experiences that are the mind known by ordinary people. The contact between the mind and the world results in the various feelings of love, hate, anger, and so on. These are *dhammas* that are even less to be grasped at or clung to than the material *dhammas*, because they are illusions born of defiled illusions. Clinging to them is extremely dangerous.

The Buddha taught that even *sati-paññā* should not be grasped at or clung to, because it is merely a part of nature. Attaching to it will give rise to fresh delusion. There will be "I who have *sati-paññā*" and there will be "my mindfulness and wisdom" arising as new attachments. The mind is weighed down with grasping and clinging. It lurches about in line with the changes that its attachments undergo and suffers *dukkha* accordingly. Knowledge should be looked on as being simply knowledge. If, deluded, one grasps at or clings to it, various kinds of attachments to rites and rituals (*sīlabbataparāmāsa*) will occur, through which one will experience *dukkha* without even noticing it.

Practicing Dhamma is similar—it's just practice. We know it as a natural truth that the results will always be in direct proportion to the practice done. The results can't be taken as "I" or "mine," either. If one grasps at or clings to practice, one falls into error again, creates another spurious self, and experiences *dukkha* no differently than if one were clinging to something as gross as sexual desire.

All Nature Is *Suññatā*

Once we reach the paths, fruits, and *nibbāna*, they too are *dhammas*, or natures, which are "just-like-that" (*tathatā*). Finally, even voidness itself is merely a natural thing. So is *nibbāna* itself, which is the same thing as voidness. If one grasps at or clings to it then it is a false *nibbāna*, a false voidness, because *nibbāna*, true voidness, is totally ungraspable. Thus, we may say that if *nibbāna* or voidness is grasped at, it's the wrong *nibbāna*, the wrong voidness. All of these examples demonstrate that there is absolutely nothing at all apart from *dhammas*.

The word *dhamma* means "nature." This interpretation is in line with the etymology of the word, for the word *dhamma* means "a thing that cherishes itself." Anything that can cherish or maintain itself is called a *dhamma*. *Dhammas* are divided into two categories: those that flow and those that do not. You won't be able to find more than just these two categories. Those that flow, spin, and change due to some concocting force maintain their existence within that very flow and change; that is, their nature is this stream of transformation itself. That which does not flow, spin, and change, because it has no causes and conditions, is *nibbāna*, or voidness, and nothing else. It is able to maintain itself without change; it is itself the state of changelessness.

The kind of *dhamma* that undergoes transformation and the kind that doesn't are both merely *dhammas*—things that maintain themselves in a certain condition. So there is nothing more than nature, nothing more than the elements of nature, only *dhammas*. How can mere *dhammas* be "I" or "mine"? In this context, *dhammas* means nature, the natural; in other words, *dhammas* are "just like that": they can't be any other way. There are only *dhammas*. "All things" are nothing but *dhammas*; there are no *dhammas* apart from "all things."

True Dhamma, no matter what aspect, topic, level, or kind, must be one with *suññatā*, completely void of self. Therefore we must look for and find *suññatā* in all things, must study voidness in all things, all *dhammas*. To speak in terms of logic:

all things = *dhammas*
all things = voidness
dhammas = voidness

We can express this in any number of ways, but the important point to understand is that there is nothing apart from nature and all nature is voidness. Nothing whatsoever should be grasped at or clung to as being "I" or "mine." So from this it can be seen clearly that voidness is the nature of all things. Only by ending every kind of delusion can *suññatā* be discerned. To see voidness there must be *paññā* that is undeluded, undefiled, pure, and true.

IGNORANCE OF *SUÑÑATĀ*

There is a further category of *dhammas*, the *dhammas* of *avijjā*, of false knowing and delusion, which are reactions arising from the contact of the mind with the world of materiality. As we said earlier, when the mind or a mental *dhamma* comes into contact with a material *dhamma*, a reaction of feeling takes place. That experience may follow either the path of ignorance (*avijjā*) or of clear, correct knowing (*vijjā*). The direction taken depends on the external conditions and the nature of that group of concocted things (*saṅkhāras*) that make up the experience. They're just more *dhammas*, *dhammas* of ignorance, causing grasping and clinging to an illusory self and to things as belonging to self. Don't forget that they're just *dhammas* and that their true essence is voidness.

Ignorance is suññatā just as much as wisdom and *nibbāna* are. If we look on them all as being dhammas equally, we will continually see their voidness of self. Dhammas of this level, even though they are one and the same thing as voidness, may still result in ignorance, may still cause the illusion of self to arise in consciousness. So we should be wary of the dhammas of the grasping and clinging kind, and the dhammas of ignorance, which are also included in all things.

If we really understand all things, this ignorant grasping and clinging won't take place. If we don't understand them and just blindly follow the influence of our animal instincts, which are stupid and deluded, we open the doors to the *dhammas* of ignorance over and over again.

We are full of grasping and clinging as if it were an inheritance that has been passed down from we don't know when. We can see that from the moment of birth we received training from those around us, some of it intentional and some unintentional, solely in the ways of ignorance, solely in the ways of grasping at self and the belongings of self. Never once were we trained in the ways of selflessness. Children never receive that sort of training. They are taught only in terms of self. Originally, at birth, a child's mind doesn't have much sense of self, but it gets stirred up by the environment. As soon as a child opens its eyes or experiences anything, it's taught to cling to that thing as being "my father," "my mother," "my home," "my food." Even the dish that the child eats from has to be "mine," no one else can use it. This unintentional process—the arising, development, and growth of the child's ego-consciousness—occurs continually, according to its own laws. By the time the child has grown into an adult, she or he is stuffed full of attachment and the mental defilements that it causes. So for us, ego *is* life, life *is* ego. When the instinct of clinging to self is the ordinary life, that life is inseparable from *dukkha*. It is heavy, oppressive, entangling, constricting, smothering, piercing, and burning—all symptoms of *dukkha*.

The *dhammas* of foolishness, delusion, and ignorance emerge continually, because our culture and the way we live encourage the *dhammas* of ego, selfishness, and ignorance. They don't encourage the *dhammas* of knowledge. Consequently, we undergo the punishment for our "original sin." We are punished when we are continually misled by our seeming autonomy and the illusion of self, without ever learning our lesson. The young aren't aware of this punishment, the middle-aged aren't aware of it, and even many of the old aren't aware of it. We should at least be able to realize it by middle age or old age so as to escape the punishment, emerge from the cage of the cycles of birth and death (*vaṭṭasaṁsāra*), and reach the boundlessness of clarity, freedom, and peace.

GOODNESS AND GRASPING

The fact is that if one grasps and clings, even to goodness, that is *dukkha*. In this sense, that which the world assumes to be goodness is actually false or evil. Goodness is still *dukkha*; it has the *dukkha* appropriate to it because it's not yet void; it's still busy and disturbed. Only when there is *suññatā*, and one is beyond goodness, can there be freedom from *dukkha*.

Therefore, the main principle of Buddhism as elucidated in the phrase "*Sabbe dhammā nālaṁ abhinivesāya*" is nothing other than the complete elimination of grasping at and clinging to things as being self or as belonging to self. There is nothing beyond this.

When we are completely identified with grasping, when we and grasping are truly the same thing, what can we do? Who can help the mind when it is in such a state? The answer to this question is nothing else but the mind itself.

We have already said that there is nothing other than *dhammas*: falseness is a *dhamma*, correctness is a *dhamma*, dukkha is a *dhamma*, the extinguishing of *dukkha* is a *dhamma*, the tool to remedy *dukkha* is a *dhamma*, the body is a *dhamma*, and the mind is a *dhamma*. Therefore, there is nothing other than *dhammas*, which must continue according to their natures, depending on mechanisms within them. What we call them—"good" or "evil"—doesn't matter.

If a certain person, when making contact with the world, increasingly develops along the lines of mindfulness and wisdom, we call that "goodness" or "virtue" (*puñña*). If another person, when making contact with the world, increasingly develops along the lines of stupidity and delusion, we call that "evil" (*pāpa*).

If we observe, we can see that nobody is born disadvantaged; each one of us is born with eyes, ears, a nose, a tongue, a body, and a mind. Outside each one of us, there are the same forms, sounds, smells, tastes, tactile sensations, and mental objects. Every one of us has the opportunity to make contact with these things, and we all contact them in exactly the same way. Why, then, do we split up into those who follow the path of foolishness, which is sinful and unwholesome, and those who follow the path of wisdom, which is virtuous and skillful?

We are fortunate that the *dhammas*, even the harmful ones, are actually a support for people. Suffering chastens us and makes us remember. We are like the child who tries to pick up fire and is unlikely to do it again, once it has seen the consequences. With material things, seeing is easy, but when it comes to picking up the fire of grasping and clinging, the fires of greed, aversion, and delusion, most of us aren't even aware that we're holding any fires at all. On the contrary, we misguidedly believe them to be lovable and desirable, and so we are never chastened. We never learn our lesson.

BURNING *DHAMMAS*

There is only one remedy, and that is to investigate the true nature of these *dhammas* until we know that THESE *DHAMMAS* ARE FIRE! They cannot be grasped at or clung to. Then we are following the path of *sati-paññā*, learning our lessons and remembering that whenever anything is grasped as "I" or "mine," the fire is ignited. It isn't a fire that burns the hand; it's a fire that consumes the mind and heart. Sometimes it burns so deep within that we aren't aware that there's a fire at all. Thus, we sink into the fiery mass that is the round of birth and death (*vaṭṭasaṁsāra*), which is the very hottest fire there is, hotter than a blast furnace. If we fail to look on things like a child who has grabbed hold of fire once and refuses to do so again, we can end up in the worst kind of furnace.

The Buddha explained that when the painful consequences of grasping and clinging are seen, the mind will relax its grip. So the question is, have we seen the painful consequences of grasping yet? If we haven't, then we haven't relaxed our grip, and if we haven't relaxed our grip, then we are not void. On another occasion, the Buddha taught that whenever one sees *suññatā*, then one finds contentment in *nibbāna*. Only when one begins to see the nonexistence of self will the mind learn to find contentment in the *āyatana* (experience) of *nibbāna*. Anything that

41

can be known through the eyes, ears, nose, tongue, body, or mind is called an *āyatana*. *Nibbāna* is called an *āyatana* here because it is merely another *dhamma* that can be experienced. How can we be so foolish as not to see it? We will be able to know it from the moment we see the state void of self, because on the relaxation of grasping and clinging, we will be content with the *āyatana* that is *nibbāna*. But it's difficult. As I've said, our life is one of constant grasping. When there is no abatement of that grasping, there is no voidness, and so no contentment in the experience of *nibbāna*.[22]

We can see the truth of this point by taking a look at other religions. Other religions do not have the term "grasping at and clinging to the words 'I' and 'mine'" (*attavādupādāna*).[23] Why is this so? Because they teach a self to be grasped at and clung to. Because they do not regard such grasping as wrong, it becomes right; in fact it becomes the goal of that religion or sect. They teach the attainment of Self. In Buddhism, however, attachment to self is specified as a defilement, as foolishness and delusion. The Buddhist practice lies in its complete relinquishment. Consequently, the complete teaching of *anattā* (not-self) is found only in Buddhism. Unlike the sects that teach a self to be grasped at or to be attained, we teach the complete destruction of the sense of self. The aim of this teaching is to perceive the state of *anattā*: the condition, found in all things, of being void of self.

Only Buddhists talk about *anattā*. Knowledge and understanding of it can arise only in those people who have been taught that all things are not-self and should never be grasped at or clung to. If one is taught that there is a self that must be grasped at and clung to, there is no way one can practice to realize the *suññatā* of self.

We must realize that just as it is necessary to see the danger of fire in order to be afraid of being burnt, so we must also see the danger of the fires of greed, aversion, and delusion—and of clinging to self, which is the root cause of all fires. Then we become gradually bored with and averse to these fires. We are able to relax our grip on them, and never think of lighting any more fires.

42

6. Void of "I" and "Mine"

NOW WE COME to the *suññatā* that, when it is seen, brings contentment in *nibbāna*. We must thoroughly understand that the first level of voidness is absence of the feelings of "I" and "mine." If those feelings are still present, the mind is not void. It is "busy" with grasping and clinging.[24] We can use the word "void" to mean freedom from the feeling of self and the sense that things belong to self. We can use the words "busy" or "disturbed" to mean confused, depressed, and in turmoil with the feelings of "I" and "mine."

What are the characteristics of being void of the "I" and "mine" feelings? In the scriptures, one teaching of the Buddha lists four items in two pairs:

> To feel that there is nothing that is "me"
>   (*Na ahaṁ kavacini*),
> Without worry or doubt that anything might be "me"
>   (*Na kassaci kiñcanaṁ kismiñci*);
> To feel that there is nothing that is "mine"
>   (*Na mama kavacini*),
> Without worry or doubt that anything might be "mine"
>   (*Kismiñci kiñcanaṁ natthi*).[25]

We may be aware that there is nothing that is "me," but sometimes there remains some anxiety that there just *might* be something that is "me." We feel that there is nothing that is mine, but we can't help doubting whether there may in fact be something that is. There must be an absolute, unshakably clear awareness that there is nothing that is self and nothing that we need to worry about as possibly being self; that there is nothing that belongs to self and nothing to wonder about, to worry over, to doubt, or to wait for, as being ours. At the moment that someone's mind is freed from these four things, there exists what the Buddha maintained is voidness. The Commentary sums it up concisely:

> Not taking things to be self
> (*Na attanena*),
> Not taking things as belonging to self
> (*Na attaniyena*).

And that is sufficient. When this ego-grasping consciousness is gone, try to imagine what there would be. One doesn't look on anything anywhere as ever having been, as currently being, or as having the potential to become self or a belonging of self. There is no self in the present and no basis for anxiety regarding self in the present, past, or future. The mind has realized *suññatā* through seeing clearly that there is nothing at all that can fulfill the meaning of the words "self" and "belonging to self." All things are *dhammas*, natural things, simply elements of nature.

Mind Is *Suññatā*

Such is the mind that is one with *suññatā*. If we say that the mind has attained or realized voidness, some people will understand that the mind is one thing and voidness another. To say that the mind comes to know voidness is still not exactly correct. Please understand that if the mind was not one and the same thing as voidness, there would be no way for voidness to be known. In its natural state, the mind is *suññatā*; an alien foolishness is what interferes with and obstructs the vision of voidness. Consequently, as soon as foolishness departs, the mind and voidness are one. The mind then knows itself. It doesn't have to go anywhere else to know anything. It holds to the knowing of voidness, knowing nothing but freedom from "self" and "belonging to self."

It is this voidness that is the single highest teaching of the Buddha, so much so that in the *Saṁyutta-nikāya* the Buddha says that there are no words spoken by the Tathāgata that are not concerned with *suññatā*. He says, in this discourse (*sutta*), that the most profound teachings are those dealing with voidness and that everything else is superficial. Only the teaching of *suññatā* is so profound that an enlightened Tathāgata must appear in the world in order to teach it. Other matters are superficial and don't require a Tathāgata's appearance.

SUÑÑATĀ FOR LAYPEOPLE

In another passage from the *Saṁyutta-nikāya*, the Buddha says that *suññatā* is the dhamma that is always of long-lasting benefit and support for laypeople. There is the account of a group of wealthy laypeople going to visit the Buddha and asking for a *dhamma* that would be of long-lasting benefit and welfare to householders, "those who are hampered by spouse and children, the wearers of sandalwood paste and perfumes."[26] In reply, the Buddha taught them this *sutta* about *suññatā*. When they objected that it was too difficult, he dropped the subject level no lower than the practices leading to "stream-entry" (*sotāpatti-yaṅka*),[27] which is the genuine realization of the Buddha, Dhamma, and Sangha, along with the virtuous conduct that is satisfying to the Noble Ones (*ariyakantasīla*). In fact, these laypeople were being lured into a trap by the Buddha. He neatly caught them in his snare. To speak in coarse, everyday terms, he swindled them. They said they didn't want *suññatā*, but the Buddha gave them something that would prevent escape from *suññatā*, the lasso that would pull them into it. For there is only one way to truly realize the Buddha, Dhamma, and Sangha, and to have the virtuous conduct that is satisfying to the Noble Ones, and that way is to continually see the futility of grasping and clinging.

Now, do you think the Buddha was wrong in saying that *suññatā* is a matter for laypeople? If he was right, then these days we must be crazy, utterly wrong, because we believe that *suññatā* is not a matter for householders, but is a matter only for those who are going to *nibbāna*, wherever that is. That's how people talk. Here the Buddha is talking in a different way, saying that this subject of *suññatā* is of direct benefit and welfare to laypeople. So who is right and who is wrong? If the Buddha is right, we must agree to investigate the truth of his words. The way to do this is to examine which people have the most suffering and distress, which people's minds are most in the middle of the blast furnace. None but laypeople. That being so, who most needs something to quench that fire, to completely destroy *dukkha* in its every aspect? Again, laypeople. Those who are in the heat of the fire must look for the means of quenching it there in its midst, because there is no place to struggle and escape to: everything is fire. Nothing exists that doesn't blaze into flames the moment it is grasped. Thus, one must find the point of absolute coolness right there in the midst of the fire. That point is voidness, freedom from self and the belongings of self—*suññatā*.

Laypeople must discover *suññatā* and dwell within its sphere. If one is unable to live right at its central point, then at the very least, one should dwell within its sphere or have a reasonable knowledge of it. Dwelling within the sphere of *suññatā* is reckoned to be of long-lasting benefit to laypeople.

This group of people asked what would be of long-lasting benefit to them. The Buddha answered, "*Dhammas* directly connected with *suññatā* transcend the world" (*Suññatāppaṭisaṃyuttā lokuttarā dhammā*). To transcend the world is to transcend the fire. To be directly connected with *suññatā* is to be void of clinging to things as self or as belonging to self. So the saying "*Dhammas* directly connected with *suññatā* transcend the world" is a gift from the Buddha especially for laypeople. The Buddha insisted on this in his own words. Please consider anew how necessary it is that we give attention to this subject. Is it not, in fact, the only subject worth discussing? In another *sutta*, the Buddha clearly

46

states that *suññatā* is *nibbāna* and that *nibbāna* is *suññatā*, freedom from defilements and *dukkha*. Therefore, *nibbāna* is a fit subject for laypeople, too. If laypeople still don't know the meaning of *nibbāna*, if they have not yet dwelt within its sphere, they must live in the midst of fire more than any other group of people.

VOID OF SUFFERING

The meaning of the word *nibbāna* is clearly defined as freedom from *dukkha* and as freedom from the mental defilements, which are the causes of *dukkha*. At any moment that our minds are void of "I" and "mine," that is *nibbāna*. For example, at this moment, as you sit reading, you probably have a mind void of the feelings of "I" and "mine," because there is nothing engendering those feelings. There are just the words you are reading for the sake of abandoning "I" and "mine." If there is some voidness (and I merely use the word "some," it's not completely or unchangeably void), then you are dwelling within the sphere of *nibbāna*. Even though it is not absolute or perfect *nibbāna*, it is *nibbāna* just the same.

Dhammas have many meanings, levels, and stages. The *dhamma* that is *nibbāna* lies in the mind of each one of you at the moment in which you are to some degree void of the sense of "I" and "mine." Please be aware of this egoless feeling; remember it well and keep it with you. Sometimes, when you arrive home, it will feel as if you've entered someone else's house. Or, doing some work at home, you will feel as if you are helping out with someone else's work, at someone else's home. This sort of feeling will increase steadily, and the *dukkha* that used to be associated with home and work will vanish. You will abide with a mind void of "I" and "mine" at all times. This is to take *nibbāna* or *suññatā* as the holy charm to hang constantly from your neck.[28] *Suññatā* is a protection against every kind of suffering, danger, and misfortune. It is the genuine holy charm of the Buddha; anything else is just a fake.

With my speaking like this, you'll soon be accusing me of giving you a big sales pitch. Don't think of me as someone hawking the Buddha's wares in the marketplace. Think rather that we are all companions in *dukkha*—in birth, old age, sickness, and death—that we are all disciples of the Lord Buddha. If anything is spoken to stimulate interest, it is with good intention. Yet those with sufficient *sati-paññā* will be able to see for themselves without having to believe me. That seeing will increasingly open the way for further study toward the ultimate truth. In this spirit of investigation, we will move our study to the subject of the *dhātus* (elements).

7. Elements of Suññatā

THE WORD *dhātu* has the same meaning as the word *dhamma*. Etymologically the words have the same root, *dhṛ*, which means "to maintain, cherish, hold, support." A *dhātu* is something that can maintain itself. Just as with *dhammas*, changing *dhātus* maintain themselves through change, and unchanging *dhātus* maintain themselves through changelessness. We ought to study these *dhātus*, which are things incapable of being self.

What sort of elements do you know that could be voidness itself, the essence of *suññatā*? Students of physics and chemistry know only the material elements, of which there are over a hundred, with more being discovered all the time. None of these elements could ever be *suññatā* itself. If we say they are *suññatā*, we mean that their deepest meaning is voidness, but they aren't *suññatā* itself, because they are merely material elements (*rūpa-dhātu*). There are also immaterial elements (*arūpa-dhātu*), elements of mind or consciousness, which lie beyond the domain of physics and chemistry. One must study the Buddha's science before one can understand the immaterial, intangible elements that are a matter of the mind and heart.

THE VOIDNESS ELEMENT

In which of these two kinds of elements does voidness abide? If a person were to say that *suññatā* is a material element, his or her friends would die laughing. Some people would say that it is an immaterial or formless element, and here the Noble Ones (*ariyā*) would die laughing. Voidness is neither a material nor an immaterial element, but is a third kind of element that lies beyond the ken of ordinary people. The Buddha called it "quenching element" or "cessation element" (*nirodha-dhātu*). The words "material element" (*vatthu-dhātu*) or "form element" (*rūpa-dhātu*) refer to materiality in visible forms, sounds, odors, tastes, or tactile objects. "Formless element" (*arūpa-dhātu*) refers to the mind and heart, to mental processes, and to the thoughts and experiences that arise in the mind. There is only one kind of element not included in these two categories, an element that is the antithesis and thorough quenching of the others. Consequently, the Buddha sometimes called it "coolness element" (*nibbāna-dhātu*), sometimes "quenching element" (*nirodha-dhātu*), and sometimes "deathless element" (*amata-dhātu*).

Nirodha-dhātu and *nibbāna-dhātu* both mean "quenching." It is the quenching element, the element that quenches all other elements. *Amata-dhātu* means "the element that does not die." All other elements die. They must die, because it is their nature to die. *Nirodha-dhātu* is not tied to birth and death; on the contrary, it is the utter quenching of the other elements. *Suññatā* is that which dwells in this element, and so it might also be called *suññatā-dhātu*, for it is the element that is the source of voidness for all other *dhātus*.

If one is to understand those things called *dhātu* well enough to understand the Dhamma, they must be studied in this way. Don't be deceived into thinking that knowing the elements of earth, water, wind, and fire is sufficient; they are just a matter for children. Those elements were already spoken of and taught about before the time of the Buddha. One must go on to know the immaterial consciousness element (*viññāna-dhātu*); the space element (*ākāsa-dhātu*); and the voidness element (*suññatā-dhātu*), which is the utter quenching of earth, water,

50

fire, wind, consciousness, and space. The element of voidness is the most wonderful element in all of Buddhism.

In short, earth, water, wind, and fire fit in the category of form element (*rūpa-dhātu*). The mind, sense-consciousness, and mental processes fit in the category of formless element (*arūpa-dhātu*). Then *nibbāna*, this voidness element (*suññatā-dhātu*), belongs in the category of quenching element (*nirodha-dhatu*). You must find a quiet time and place to sit and look at all the elements. You will see clearly that there are only these three kinds. Then you will begin to discover *suññatā-dhātu* or *nibbāna-dhātu* and will understand this *anattā* or *suññatā* that we are discussing here.

We may lay down the principle that, in grasping at and clinging to "I" and "mine," there are form elements (*rūpa-dhātu*) and formless elements (*arūpa-dhātu*). In the absence of clinging to "I" and "mine," there is the cessation or quenching element (*nirodha-dhātu*). Conversely, one may say that if the quenching element appears, one sees only *suññatā*. The state free of "I" and "mine" manifests itself clearly. If any other element enters, one will see it as form, name, visible object, sound, smell, taste, tactile object, feeling, memory, thought, consciousness, and so on. Each one in the whole confusing crowd has a part to play in the arising of clinging—which can appear as love or else as hate.

We all have just two dominant moods: satisfaction and dissatisfaction. We are familiar with only these two. We have been interested only in gaining that which is felt to be desirable and in fleeing from or destroying that which is felt to be disagreeable. Things are unceasingly busy, and the disturbed mind is never void. What must we do to make it void? For it to be void, we must overcome or go beyond all those busy elements and come to dwell with the element of *suññatā*.

BEYOND ALL ELEMENTS

The Buddha used another threefold division to show the properties of the elements. First is the element of renunciation (*nekkhama-dhātu*), the cause for withdrawal from sensuality; second is the nonmaterial

51

element (*arūpa-dhātu*), the cause for withdrawal from materiality; and third is the element of quenching (*nirodha-dhātu*), the cause for withdrawal from the conditioned or the concocted (*saṅkhata*). Seeing the element of renunciation (*nekkhama-dhātu*) causes us to withdraw from sensuality because it is sensuality's antithesis. Seeing the element that is the opposite of sensuality is called "seeing the renunciation element." Sensuality is a fire; "not being consumed by the fire of sensuality" is the meaning of the element of renunciation. The mind that withdraws from sensuality is a mind that contains this particular element.

Once beings are able to free themselves from sensuality, they attach themselves to the beautiful and pleasurable things that, while unconnected with gross sensuality, are still in the realm of form or materiality, albeit on a refined level. For example, there are seers (*rishis*), sages (*munis*), and adepts (*yogis*) who get attached to the pleasures of meditative absorption into objects of fine-materiality (*rūpajhāna*). Or, on a more mundane level, perhaps we may see old people who are attached to antiques or exquisite potted plants. Although these things are unconnected with the crudest sensuality, such people may be even more lost than those absorbed in gross pleasures, such as lust. They are attached to material form and unable to give it up. To get free of finer materiality, we must understand the formless element (*arūpa-dhātu*), the *dhātu* that is above form.

And what will one get stuck in if one can get free from attachment to materiality? One will get caught in those causally conditioned things that surpass it, namely, all the beneficial *dhammas*. We don't have to talk of the harmful *dhammas* here: nobody wants them. But people dream endlessly about the virtues and virtuous actions that make us into wonderful people or earn us rebirth up in heaven. Nevertheless, being born in heaven is a conditioned state (*saṅkhata*). We are all caught up in being this and that self, and having these and those possessions of self. Being the self of an animal is no good, so we want a human self. Seeing that being a human is no good, we want to become a celestial being. That's no good, so we want to become a Brahma god. Seeing that being a Brahma god is no good, we want to become a Mahābrahma god. In every case, there's always a self; it's all concocted (*saṅkhata*). Only by penetrating the quenching element (*nirodha-dhātu*) can we withdraw from the conditioned and concocted.

The quenching element (*nirodha-dhātu*) is *nibbāna-dhātu*, the final element, the element of perfect peace. It is the utter quenching of "I" and "mine." If there is absolute and final quenching, one becomes an Arahant, and that's called "the element of coolness with no fuel left" (*anupādisesa-nibbāna-dhātu*). If the quenching is not yet final, one becomes one of the lesser Noble Ones (*ariyā*). That quenching is called "the element of coolness with some fuel left" (*sa-upādisesa-nibbāna-dhātu*). In this case, there is still a remnant of ego; it is not yet ultimate voidness.

To summarize, we must know the *dhātus*, the true constituents of all things. Please understand them according to the fundamental principle that there is the element with form (*rūpa-dhātu*), the element without form (*arūpa-dhātu*), and the element that is the extinguishing of both the form and formless elements (*nirodha-dhātu*). We can confidently assert that there is nothing outside the scope of these three types of elements.

We are learning something about the Buddha's science, which encompasses the physical, mental, and spiritual spheres. It enables us to have an utterly thorough knowledge of all things, which precludes any further grasping at them. Perfect nongrasping must be the meaning of *suññatā*.

8. Knowing Suññatā

Now I would like to turn to the matter of "living with *suññatā*," or dwelling in voidness. To consider this subject, we must look at the meanings of a number of words in detail. In particular, let's focus on the words "to know," "to see clearly," "to realize," "to live with," and "to be void." Speaking in everyday language, we can make the following equations:

we know = we know *suññatā*
we see clearly = we see *suññatā* clearly
we realize = we realize *suññatā*
we live with = we live with *suññatā*
we are void = we are void through *suññatā*—we are voidness itself

REALLY KNOWING

Most people might think that the phrase "we know *suññatā*" means that we have studied and discussed it. If that's all our knowing is, we don't know voidness correctly. The words "to know" in Dhamma language don't refer to the knowing that comes from study, listening, and the like. Such knowing, even if we say that we understand, is not complete. The words "to know" and "to understand" in ordinary, everyday language are merely a matter of reading and listening, of thinking and reasoning. Those activities can't be used to know voidness. The "knowing of *suññatā*" refers to the awareness of *suññatā* in a mind that is truly void. We must know what is actually occurring in the mind. For there to be the knowing of voidness, voidness must be apparent at that moment. Then we know how it is. This, then, is called "knowing *suññatā*."

Hearing a talk or reading about *suññatā*, and then considering logically that voidness should be possible, or that it may be like this or like that, is still not what is meant here by "knowing." This is merely the knowing and understanding of worldly language. When the words "to know" are used here, please take them in the particular sense they have in the Dhamma principles of Buddhism.

To know Dhamma means that Dhamma is truly present and that we are aware of it. Similarly, to know *suññatā* means that voidness is manifest in awareness. So I encourage you, in any moment that the mind has any measure of voidness, even if it's not absolutely or perfectly void, to keep recognizing it. Actually, on any one day *suññatā* is there repeatedly. Even if it's not a fixed, absolute *suññatā*, it's still very good, as long as we take the trouble to observe it. If we take an interest in this sort of voidness right from the start, it will generate a contentment with voidness that will make it easy to practice and attain the real thing. Therefore, the phrase "we know *suññatā*" refers to having voidness manifest in awareness.

The phrase "clearly seeing *suññatā*" must also be increasingly clear and precise. When we have become aware of the mind's voidness, we contemplate it. We focus our awareness on it until there is a clear penetrative seeing, a thorough understanding of voidness.

The meaning of the phrase "we realize *suññatā*" is once again the same. It refers to the moment the mind realizes voidness. In conventional terms we say that "we" realize voidness, but in fact it's the mind that realizes it. That awareness is the "one who" experiences and realizes *suññatā*.

Then the phrase "living with *suññatā*" refers to *suññatā-vihāra*. Living and breathing with the constant awareness of voidness is called "living with *suññatā*."

The phrase "being void" means that there is no feeling of "self" or "belonging to self"; there is no feeling of "I" and "mine." These feelings are the creations of craving and grasping. Being void of these feelings is "being void." What is it that is void? Once again it is the mind that is void, emptied of the feelings of "self" and of "belonging to self," in both their crude and their subtle forms. In the crude forms we call them "ego" and "egoism." In the subtle forms we call them "self" and "of self." If the mind is void to the degree of being free of even the refined self, it is said that the mind is itself *suññatā*. This agrees with the teachings of some other Buddhist traditions, which say that mind is voidness, voidness is mind; voidness is Buddha, Buddha is voidness; voidness is Dhamma, Dhamma is voidness. There is only this one thing.

TWO KINDS OF *SUÑÑATĀ*

All the myriad things we are acquainted with are nothing but *suññatā*. Let us make this clear by looking into the word "void" once more. The words *suñña* (void) and *suññatā* (voidness) point to two things, or rather, two characteristics (*lakkhaṇa*).[29]

First, *suññatā* refers to the characteristic or fundamental nature of all things. Please concentrate on the fact that the character of all things is voidness. This phrase "all things" must be understood correctly as encompassing every single thing, both physical things (*rūpadhamma*) and mental things (*nāmadhamma*), everything from a speck of dust to valuable things, to immaterial things, up to *nibbāna*. Each and every thing has the quality of voidness. This is the first meaning of *suññatā*.

We must understand well that in a speck of dust there is voidness of self. Gold, silver, and diamonds have voidness of self as their essence. Going on to the mind and heart, thoughts and feelings, each thing is characterized by *suññatā*. That is, they are void of self. The study and practice of Dhamma share the quality of being void of self. Finally, the path realizations, their fruits, and *nibbāna* itself all have this exact same property of *suññatā*. It's just that we don't see it. Even a sparrow flying back and forth has the characteristic of voidness perfectly within it, but we don't see it.

Please think this over. Contemplate it, observe it, and ponder it until you perceive that all things display the characteristic of *suññatā*. It's just that we can't see. So who is to blame but ourselves? There's a Zen koan that says, "An ancient pine tree is proclaiming the Dhamma." Even that old pine tree is displaying *suññatā*, the voidness that it shares with all things, but people don't see it. They don't hear its Dhamma teaching, its ceaseless proclamation of voidness. This, then, is the word *suññatā* in its first meaning, which concerns all things.

The word *suññatā* in its second application points to the quality of the mind when it isn't grasping and clinging at anything. The character of the mind when it isn't attaching to anything is called "voidness" also. The first meaning of *suññatā* points out that all things are void, that voidness is the inherent characteristic of all things. The second meaning points to the mind that isn't grasping or clinging at anything.

Ordinarily, although it is truly void of self, the mind doesn't realize that it is void, because it is constantly enveloped and disturbed by conceptual thoughts, which are concocted due to seeing, hearing, smelling, tasting, and physical experiencing. Consequently, the mind is aware neither of its own voidness nor of the voidness in all things. However, when the mind completely throws off the things enveloping it, when it removes the grasping and clinging caused by delusion and ignorance, then the mind has the character of *suññatā* through its nonclinging.

The two sorts of *suññatā*, the voidness of the nonclinging mind and the voidness of all things, are different but related. Because all things truly have the characteristic of being void of self, and because they are void of any permanent, independent entity to be grasped at or clung to, we are able to see the truth of their voidness. If in fact they weren't void of self, then it would be impossible to see that they are void.

As it is, although all things are void, we see every one of them as not-void. The mind enveloped by defilement and ignorance attaches to everything as being self, no matter what it is. Even a tiny particle of dust is regarded as the self of that dust. It is experienced as a "second person," which stands apart from ourselves. We are the "first person," and the "second person" is everything else. We label others as being this and being that, always seeing them as being permanent, independent entities, thus, as separate selves.

Therefore, we must know correctly, absolutely, and perfectly the meaning of the word *suñña* (void). Know that, first, it is the essence of all things and, second, it is the character of the nonclinging mind. The first voidness is an object of knowledge or realization. The second voidness is this void mind, the quality of the mind that is void through realizing the truth of *suññatā*. It's the result of correct Dhamma practice. Thus, the mind that sees *suññatā* in all things disintegrates of itself, leaving only voidness. It becomes voidness itself and sees everything as void, everything from a speck of dust up to and including *nibbāna*. Material objects, people, animals, place, time, space—whatever they may be—all *dhammas* melt into one, into *suññatā*, through the knowing of this truth. This is the meaning of the words *suñña* and *suññatā*.

REMAINDERLESS QUENCHING

It should now be clear that the word "void" is equivalent to the remainderless quenching of ego and egoism—the total cessation of the experience of "I" and "mine." Void is the same as the total quenching of self.

The self is merely a condition that arises when there is grasping and clinging in the mind. We don't see it as void, but we see it as self, because of our grasping and clinging through ignorance and desire. So, without intending to, we cling. Because the mind doesn't know better, grasping arises by itself. Not that we make a deliberate effort or conscious attempt to establish this or that as a self—when the mind contains ignorance, it inevitably experiences all things as being or having selves, without requiring deliberate will or intention.

If correct understanding occurs, so that all things are seen as they truly are, we will see the truth that *suññatā* is the remainderless quenching of self. Thus, we may state the fundamental principle that "void" means the remainderless quenching of self. That being so, we must give some attention to correctly understanding the phrase "remainderless quenching."[30]

What quenching has a remainder and what quenching doesn't have a remainder? The cessation that has a remainder represents a mere change of shape or form. Although one form is extinguished, there remains the germ of a new one. There is still endless grasping and clinging in the mind, first at this thing and then at that thing.

The *sati-paññā*, or knowledge of Dhamma, that has not yet reached its peak can quench only some types of grasping, only some aspects of clinging some of the time. Some people may see that dust is not self but see a sparrow as being self. Others may see that trees and animals are not selves but take people to be so. In seeing people as independent entities or as selves, some will say that the body is not self but that the mind is. This is called incomplete cessation; some aspects are extinguished but others are always left behind as self. One may realize that the mind is not self but still take certain qualities of the mind, such as virtue, to be self. Or one may believe that if all these things are not self, then that which is beyond time, eternal, and unchanging—the *nibbāna*-element—is self. This sort of extinguishing always leaves a seed. Whenever we sweep out the whole lot, even the *nibbāna*-element, as not self, that is called the true remainderless quenching of self and ego.

Therefore, the phrase "the remainderless quenching of ego" means the nonarising of ego-consciousness. But this must be practiced, which means we must prevent the arising of ego. To practice consistently in this manner may also be called the remainderless quenching of ego. Correct or impeccable practice refers to practice whereby ego-consciousness has no way of arising again. In other words, we don't allow it to arise at any moment.

The Meaning of Birth

What has been said thus far provides a basis for understanding the phrase "the birth of ego." Here, "birth" (*jāti*) doesn't mean birth from a mother's womb; it means birth within the confines of the mind's concepts and thoughts. Whether you call it "relinking" or "being reborn," it must refer only to taking birth or being born within the mind's experience.

When we feel that "I am I," where is it experienced? Please understand that it arises in the mind. Birth happens there. Thus, this "birth" is not the physical birth of a flesh-and-blood body. We must understand that physical birth, even though the body already has emerged from the womb, may be considered utterly meaningless until there is a mental birth, a birth of ego-consciousness: "I am I." The body is nothing but a lump of matter until there is grasping and clinging to self. At that moment the birth of that lump of flesh is complete. That is, inwardly, there is the sense of being self.

Therefore, the true meaning of birth is defined as this sense of being self. After a child is born physically, in the moment that self-consciousness arises in it, "the child" is said to be born. As soon as that feeling is absent, "the child dies" and reverts to being a lump of flesh once more. As long as there are no other feelings that are able to stimulate the creation of self, we cannot say that "the child is born." It's as if the child were dead. Then, all of a sudden, at any moment, if some sense object, something, makes contact, then self-consciousness arises again. Thus, "the child" is born again, and then shortly afterward "the child" dies again. So we say that in a single day one is born many times. However, if one lives in such a way as to prevent self-consciousness from arising, one is not reborn. One lives in *suññata*.

9. Levels of Suññatā

IN THE *Uppaṇṇasaka-sutta* the Buddha calls *suññatā* "the abode of the Great Person" (*mahāpurisavihāra*). Voidness is where the Great Person lives.[31] The Great Person does not have a wandering, restless mind that spins this way and that like the mind of an ordinary person. The Great Person has a mind that dwells in voidness, lives with voidness, or is itself voidness. That being so, *suññatā* is the abode or home of Great Persons: the Buddha and the Arahants. To say that voidness is their abode means that they live it and breathe it.

The Buddha stated that he, the Tathāgata, lived and abided in the dwelling or house of voidness (*suññatavihāra*).[32] When he was teaching Dhamma, his mind was void of self and belonging to self. When he went on alms round or about his daily tasks, his mind was void. When he was resting in the day time (*divāvihāra*) or enjoying himself in his free time (*sukhavihāra*), he dwelt void of self and belonging to self. Consequently, he declared to Sariputta that the Tathāgata spent his life in the house of voidness (*suññatavihāra*).

Here we are not talking about the ordinary unenlightened person, but of the Great Person, of the Buddha, of how he lived and in what abode he dwelt. If you want to see the Buddha's dwelling place, don't look for a building made of bricks and mortar in India. You should think of the abode called "the house of voidness" (*suññatavihāra*) or

63

"the home of the Great Person" (*mahāpurisavihāra*). But don't forget that it must be supreme voidness (*paramaṁ suññaṁ*).

UNSURPASSABLE *SUÑÑATĀ*

The supreme *suññatā* is not the momentary flash that we all may experience sitting here, which will disappear in a little while. The Buddha's house of voidness refers to ultimate voidness, and a rather long Pali word is used for it, *paramānuttarasuññatā*. This word is composed of three words, *parama* + *anuttara* + *suññatā*, and means "supreme unsurpassable voidness." The term is related, in the technical literature of Dhamma, to the concentration of mind (*cetosamādhi*) that is signless,[33] such that the mind is free and void of eruptions (*āsava*). The signless concentration of mind (*animitta cetosamādhi*), which is purified of the eruptions, may be of two kinds: the kind in which regression is possible and the kind that is permanent. If, at any moment, there is the kind of mental concentration (*cetosamādhi*) in which there are no signs to be clung to as self or as belonging to self, then that radiant mind, free of eruptions (*āsava*), is called "supreme unsurpassable voidness" (*paramānuttarasuññatā*). This is the natural, unforced state of the Arahants.

If we unenlightened people are ever going to be true adepts (*yogis*), we must be able to realize this concentration of mind. Even if we don't end the eruptions (*āsava*) once and for all, there can be occasional freedom from them. We may borrow something of the Buddha and the Arahants to try out so that we don't lose heart. That which is called voidness, liberation, or *nibbāna* can be of two kinds: the sort that is absolute and final, and the sort that is up and down, temporary, and uncertain. It is this latter sort that we ordinary folk may know. For example, at times when our surroundings are particularly fitting, the mind may be void for an hour or two. Though the voidness we experience is temporary, the important thing is that we intend to practice making the mind void to the best of our abilities.

The term "supreme unsurpassable voidness" (*paramānuttara-suññatā*), as used by the Buddha, means the utter destruction of greed, hatred, and delusion. It is the complete destruction of grasping at and clinging to things as self or as belonging to self. It has the same meaning as "final abandonment" (*samuccheda-pahāna*). Consequently, when speaking of the highest level of *suññatā* the Buddha used this term "supreme unsurpassable voidness."

STEPS OF SUÑÑATĀ

If we gradually lower our eyes from the summit of *suññatā*, we will be able to understand the lesser levels of voidness. Directly below the peak of supreme unsurpassable voidness (*paramānuttara-suññatā*) are the following:

> Experience that is neither-experience-nor-nonexperience
> (*nevasaññānāsaññāyatana*)
> Experience of infinite nothingness (*ākiñcaññāyatana*)
> Experience of infinite consciousness (*viññāṇañcāyatana*)
> Experience of infinite space (*ākāsānañcāyatana*)
> Recognition of "just earth" (*pathavīsaññā*)
> Recognition of "just forest" (*araññasaññā*)

Looking downward from the summit, these things are hard to understand, so we will start from the bottom and gradually raise our eyes up to the peak.[34]

The first level is the recognition of "just forest" (*araññasaññā*), which means the recognition of forest. If where we live is noisy and confusing, imagine it to be a forest, just as if it truly were one and we really have entered it. Imagine the forest to be void and tranquil, free from all disturbing noises. Merely imagining a forest is already to get one sort of voidness, a voidness that is child's play.

Higher than the recognition of "just forest" (*araññasaññā*) is the recognition of "just earth" (*pathavīsaññā*), whereby we create the perception or recognition of earth. We recognize all phenomena as being merely the earth element. The recognition of earth can eradicate sensual

65

passion regarding visible forms, sounds, odors, tastes, and tactile objects. It is something that young men and women should try.

Here, if we wish to ascend further, we must create the feeling that there is nothing but infinite space (*ākāsānañcāyatana*). Space is indeed one kind of voidness, but it is not yet *suññatā*. *Suññatā* is of a higher order than vacant, empty space. Don't be interested in that sort of emptiness. Pay attention to the more subtle level of *suññatā* whereby we create the perception that there is nothing but endless consciousness. The perception that there is nothing but the endlessness of the consciousness-element is called *viññāṇañcāyatana*. If we ascend even higher, we reach the kind of voidness called *ākiñcaññāyatana* whereby we mentally create utter nothingness. We don't allow the mind to focus on anything, we fix it on nothingness; however, there still remains the experience that there is nothingness.

One step further lies the experience that is neither experience nor nonexperience (*nevasaññānāsaññāyatana*), which is experiencing through nonexperience. It is said that it is neither like being alive nor like being dead. To say that there is experience would be false. To say that there is no experience would also be false. There is no recognition, labeling, or interpretation of experience. There is awareness without recognition. This state is so subtle that to call a person in it "alive" would be false, and to call him "dead" would be false. This too is a kind of voidness.

These six levels of voidness are not the same as supreme unsurpassable voidness (*paramānuttarasuññatā*). The Buddha spoke of them merely to demonstrate the various gradations of voidness. None of them are the voidness that is the abode of the Great Person. They are the sorts of voidness that seekers and sages had been groping after since before the time of the Buddha. Having discovered such things, the old meditators always got stuck and were unable to go beyond them. This was the case until the Buddha found the true *suññatā*, which is the abode of the Great Person, the supreme unsurpassable voidness of which I have been speaking.

In Touch with *Suññata*

The Commentaries call the experience of *suññata* "void contact" (*suññataphassa*). We know only the ordinary contacts (*phassa*) of the eyes, ears, nose, tongue, body, and mind with visible forms, sounds, odors, tastes, tangible objects, and mental objects. We hardly ever have contact with *suññata*, because we know only the form element (*rupa-dhatu*) and the formless element (*arupa-dhatu*); we know nothing of the element of quenching (*nirodha-dhatu*).

When we come to know the quenching element (*nirodha-dhatu*), we will have a new experience, what the commentators call "void contact" (*suññataphassa*). This is a name for the contact taking place at the level of Noble Path, which truly destroys mental defilements. When we have developed the path to the point at which it is destroying defilement, then there is void contact (*suññataphassa*). It is like touching *suññata* with our hands; our minds come into contact with voidness. The voidness contacted here refers to the Noble Path of one who is continually developing the contemplation of not-self (*anattanupassana*), seeing that there is neither self nor anything belonging to self, seeing that there are merely dhammas and natural processes. This Noble Path is called *suññato*, and any contact that takes place on that Path is called *suññataphassa*.

Contemplation of not-self (*anattanupassana*), the cause of void contact, develops from insight into *dukkha* (*dukkhanupassana*). Contemplation of *dukkha* is like having once tried to take hold of fire, having found it painfully hot, and then knowing that fire is not at all something to grab. In the same way, we know that any *dhamma* we grab becomes a fire. Then we know that no *dhammas* whatsoever should be grabbed—that is, grasped at or clung to. The spiritual experience of how fire burns, scorches, consumes, constricts, envelops, pierces, and entangles is spiritual insight into *dukkha* (*dukkhanupassana*). It leads to spiritual experiences of not-self (*anattanupassana*) and voidness (*suññatanupassana*), so this kind of contact or experience is called "void contact" (*suññata-phassa*).

67

Here we must consider the objection of some people that if one hasn't reached *nibbāna*, one can't know anything about it, just as one can't have seen Europe if one has never been there. However, *nibbāna* is not some material thing; it is experienced by mind, in the heart, through consciousness. There are many moments when mind is naturally free or void, like a free sample from nature. As you pay attention to this teaching, most of your minds are probably free-void. Though just a taste of *nibbāna*, be diligent in contemplating it.

LIBERATED INTO VOIDNESS

In our practice of mindfulness with breathing (*ānāpānasati*), one area focuses on the careful scrutiny of mind's reality (*cittānupassanā*). One approach to doing so, while breathing in and out, is to use perspectives on mind such as the following:

> If the mind has lust, know that the mind has lust.
> If the mind has hatred, know that the mind has hatred.
> If the mind has delusion, know that the mind has delusion.
> If the mind is depressed, know that the mind is depressed.
> If the mind is not depressed, know that the mind is not depressed.
> If the mind is liberated, know that the mind is liberated.
> If the mind is not liberated, know that the mind is not liberated.[35]

If the mind is liberated, then it is void. If it is not liberated, then it is not void. Let us now look at our mind that is either liberated, that is, void of all things, or else caught, grasping and clinging to something. Even at the initial level of practice, the teaching is to look at the mind that is void or liberated. Liberation or deliverance (*vimutti*) is something to be seen within, not to be figured out or guessed at according to the books we've read.

Nibbāna or *suññatā* is right here for us to see, even while we are still ordinary worldly people, for there is the voidness called "coincidental deliverance" (*tadaṅga-vimutti*). This is voidness that just happens to arise, as it can right now, when external conditions are right. A second type of voidness can arise when we concentrate the mind in the correct way, so that it's completely undisturbed and at ease—more so than when experiencing any kind of worldly pleasure. This is deliverance through suppression (*vikkhambhana-vimutti*). A third type, cut-off-at-the-roots deliverance (*samuccheda-vimutti*), is the final release of the Arahant. Even without this final deliverance, we still have a sample of *suññatā* to examine, a sample of the Buddha's wares. If you are interested, you can find such a free sample in yourself.

Therefore, we should practice mindfulness with breathing stage by stage, developing the contemplations of the body (*kāyānupassanā*), of the feelings (*vedanānupassanā*), of the mind (*cittānupassanā*), and of Dhamma (*dhammānupassanā*).[36] Mindfulness with breathing is a continuous tasting of *suññatā* from start to finish. Finally, one understands voidness through seeing the painful consequences of grasping and clinging. Then the mind will immediately turn to find contentment with the experience (*āyatana*) of *nibbāna*.

We are able to see *suññatā* continually, step-by-step, before actually reaching its supreme level. There is a progression that follows its own law, which is the law of nature itself. When one comprehends something by oneself, the resulting knowledge is firm. It does not sway and totter like the knowledge gained by listening to others or like deluded knowledge.

As for happiness, we don't have to do anything much to make ourselves happy. We needn't go to any great trouble; all we must do is to void our minds of greed, hatred, and delusion. In other words, make it void of grasping at and clinging to "I" and "mine." When the mind is void of greed, hatred, and delusion, it's truly void, and all *dukkha* comes to an end. Even action (*kamma*) will, of itself, come to an end.

VOIDING *KAMMA*

In the *Aṅguttara-nikāya*, the Buddha states that when the mind is void of greed, hatred, and delusion, is void of "I" and "mine," then *kamma* ends by itself.[37] This means that *kamma*, its result (*vipāka*), and the mental defilements that are the causes for the creation of kamma, spontaneously and simultaneously come to an end. We needn't fear *kamma*, thinking that we must be ruled by our *kamma*. We needn't be interested in *kamma*. Rather, we should take an interest in *suññatā*. If we make "I" and "mine" void, *kamma* will utterly disintegrate and will have no power to make us follow its dictates.

For this reason, someone like Aṅgulīmāla, the murderer, could become an Arahant.[38] Please don't explain Aṅgulīmāla's story wrongly, as is often done. He did not become an Arahant merely by not killing. The Buddha said to Aṅgulīmāla, "I have stopped. You have not stopped." Please don't say that "not stopped" means that Aṅgulīmāla was still killing people and that he became an Arahant because he stopped murdering. Anyone who explains the story like that is badly misrepresenting the Buddha. When the Buddha used the word "stop" here, he was referring to the stopping of "I" and "mine," to the stopping of grasping and clinging. In short, voidness is "stopping" and only this kind of stopping could make Aṅgulīmāla an Arahant. If to stop murdering is all it took, why aren't all people who don't kill Arahants? Why aren't we all Arahants? True stopping is the voidness in which there is no self to dwell anywhere, to come or go anywhere, to do anything. This is true stopping. If there is still a self, then you can't "stop."

So we should understand that the word "void" has the same meaning as "stop," the single word by which the Buddha turned Aṅgulīmāla into an Arahant, even though the killer's hands were still red with blood and his neck was still hung with the 999 finger bones of his victims. For *kamma* to end by itself, to really stop, we must rely on this single word: *suññatā*, being void of "I" and "mine," not grasping at or clinging to any *dhammas*.

YOGA OF VOIDNESS

The Buddha taught that *yoga* means "seeing the noble truth" (*ariyasacca-dassana*). Therefore, the activity of making the mind void may be called "Buddhist *yoga*." Although the *Vedanta*[39] tradition is concerned with the realization of an ultimate self, we can borrow from it the term *rāja yoga*, which means the highest level or summit of *yoga* (spiritual endeavor). However, in the Buddhist teachings, *yoga* refers to the realization of voidness, to making *suññatā* manifest. Any action that leads to the manifestation of voidness may be called *yoga*, but the word must be understood in this manner for it to be Buddhist *yoga*. It means "making the ultimate truth evident."[40] We should use this *yoga* in every mental action, so as to stop all grasping at and clinging to "I" and "mine."

Thus, we borrow the word *yoga* from another tradition and adapt its meaning appropriately. Take, for example, the *Vedanta* term *karma yoga* (*yoga* of action). It means being unselfish, acting unreservedly for the benefit of others. We Buddhists, too, have this *yoga*. If there is no ego-consciousness, whatever we do will be *karma yoga*. Even with more basic *yoga*, such as making merit, doing good, sacrificing for others, and helping mankind, all actions must be performed with a mind void of "I" and "mine." Everything becomes *yoga* when done without "I" and "mine." We needn't seek after other kinds of *yoga*, for they all come down to this one *yoga*, the spiritual endeavor of putting an end to self and the belongings of self. They all come down to manifesting *suññatā*.

SEARCH FOR THE PEARL

When Buddhism spread to China, the Chinese of those days were intelligent and clever enough to accept it. Eventually, there arose teachings such as those of Hui Neng[41] and Huang Po, which explained mind, Dhamma, Buddha, the Way, and voidness in just a few words, so that people could understand. A typical first sentence from their teaching might point out that mind, Buddha, Dhamma, the Way, and voidness are all just one thing. Just this is enough; there is no need to say anything more. One sentence is equivalent to all the scriptures. However, we may not understand. It's especially hard for those of us studying and practicing in the old style, because we have no way at all of understanding such a statement. We ought to feel a little ashamed on this account. Then our understanding would grow more quickly.

Further, the Chinese Buddhists said that voidness is by nature always present, but we don't see it. Similarly, I will say that everyone at this moment has a mind that is by nature void. But not only do we not see it; what's more, we will not accept that this is *suññatā*.

Huang Po scolded us for being like someone who, without knowing it, has a pearl attached to his forehead, yet goes searching all around the world for that same pearl. Perhaps we'll even search outside the world into the hells, heavens, and the Brahma worlds. Not seeing what is stuck to our foreheads, we seek all around the world, and if that's not enough, in the other realms. So please, just for a while, look very closely to see what is there on your forehead and how you are going to get your hands on it.

When speaking of the way to grope for the pearl, the Chinese teachers spoke even more profoundly. The Chinese Zen masters said that there's no need to do anything. Just be still and the mind will become void by itself. These words, "Just be still, there's no need to do anything," have many meanings. Our minds are naughty and playful. They wander about the eyes, ears, nose, tongue, and body gathering sense objects. Having let them in, we are stupid enough to allow ignorant *dhammas* to climb into the driver's seat, so that there is nothing but grasping and clinging to "I" and "mine." This is called being naughty, refusing to be still.

"Being still" means not admitting sense objects into the mind, being content to let them founder like waves on the shore. For instance, when the eye sees a form, if there is merely seeing, that is called "not admitting visible forms into the mind." If you can't do that and feelings of satisfaction or dissatisfaction (*vedanā*) arise, stop right there. Don't begin desiring according to those feelings. If the wave stops there, the mind has a chance to be still. But if we act to extend a feeling of satisfaction, in a moment "I" and "mine" emerge. Or if we act in response to a feeling of dissatisfaction, there will be *dukkha*. Either way, it is called "not being still."

The "being still" of the Zen masters refers to the very practice that the Buddha taught: seeing that nothing whatsoever should be grasped at or clung to as being "I" or "mine." "Being still" is identical in meaning to "*sabbe dhammā nālaṁ abhinivesāya.*" If there is nothing whatsoever to be clung to, what possible purpose can there be in busying and confusing ourselves, in rushing about things and disturbing them, rather than just "being still"?

We must look for *suññatā*, which is truly worthy of our aspiration. To say that there is a kind of voidness that gives rise to cessation, purity, clarity, or peace is still to be speaking in conventional terms. Truly speaking, there is nothing other than voidness; there is only this one thing. And voidness is not the cause of anything. It *is* Buddha; it *is* Dhamma; it *is* Sangha; it *is* the Way. It *is* purity, clarity, and peace. All these things are there as *suññatā*. If we still say that voidness is the cause of this or that, we show that we haven't yet reached supreme voidness, because if we have reached the supreme, we don't have to do anything. By being still, there is Buddha, Dhamma, Sangha, purity, clarity, peace, *nibbāna*—anything, everything—in that immutable, unconcocted state.

Huang Po had an extremely simple method for teaching people how to recognize *suññatā*. He gave them the riddle, "Look at the mind of a child before its conception." I would like to present you with this puzzle. Look at the child's mind before the child is conceived in the womb. Where is it? If you can find it, you will be able to find voidness easily, just as if you were grabbing the pearl that's already there on your forehead.

PART III

Practicing with Voidness

Nothing whatsoever should be clung to as "I" or "mine."

10. Contemplating Dependent Co-origination

WE HAVE DISCUSSED THE SPIRITUAL DISEASE from which we all suffer, and we have examined the nature of *suññatā*, which provides our cure. Now we will consider the steps we can take to treat our disease. Both in protecting against the disease and in its treatment, there must be the principle of allowing no involvement with "I" and "mine." But how is one to go about it? There are many methods.

With physical and mental diseases, one ailment can be treated in a variety of ways. We need not rely on a single fixed method, but whatever the method, the aim and the result must be the same—good health. Similarly, in treating the spiritual disease, the Buddha taught a great number of practices in order to answer the needs of different people, times, places, and occasions. So we have heard of a great number of practices with many names, and perhaps we have been frightened to hear that he established eighty-four thousand subjects of Dhamma (*dhammakhanda*). Now, if there were truly eighty-four thousand topics, we would all feel discouraged. We would die before we learned them all; nobody can learn them all. We would learn some, forget, and then have to learn them again, only to forget again, or else they would get completely mixed up in our minds. Fortunately, there is merely one handful, merely one subject, which the Buddha summarized in the one phrase, "Nothing whatsoever should be clung to as 'I' or 'mine.'" To hear this subject is to hear all subjects. To practice it is to practice everything. And to receive its fruit is to be cured of all disease.

Every one of the many methods for wiping out the disease of "I" and "mine" works. Which one you use depends on how you wish to practice.

Dependent Co-arising

One way is to constantly contemplate "I" and "mine" as illusions or hallucinations (*māyā*). This practice will enable you to see that the feeling of self, a seemingly solid entity that we are familiar with as "I" and "mine," is in fact a mere illusion. This insight is achieved by contemplating self in terms of dependent co-origination (*paṭicca-samuppāda*).

To explain *paṭicca-samuppāda* theoretically or technically takes a long time. It could take one or two months to cover just this single issue. This is because, in the field of theory, it's been turned increasingly into a psychological and philosophical subject, so that it has reached a state of excessive complexity. Yet, in the field of practice, *paṭicca-samuppāda* is, as the Buddha said, just a single handful. When there is contact with a form, sound, odor, flavor, or other sense object at one of the sense doors, that contact is called *phassa* in Pali. This phassa conditions feeling (*vedanā*). *Vedanā* conditions craving (*taṇhā*). *Taṇhā* conditions clinging (*upādāna*). *Upādāna* conditions becoming (*bhava*). Bhava conditions *jāti*, which is "birth", and following from birth there is old age, sickness, and death, which are *dukkha*.

Please see that as soon as consciousness (*viññāṇa*) meets with a sense object there is sense contact, and that the subsequent conditioning of *vedanā, taṇhā*, and so on, is called *paṭicca-samuppāda*. Dependent co-origination is the process by which various things—existing in dependence on other things through the influence of ignorance (*avijjā*)—condition the arising of new things, which in turn condition the development of further things, and so on and on. This process or stream is called *paṭicca-samuppāda*. It is a dependent co-arising wherein no self is to be found, merely dependence followed by arising. *Paṭicca-samuppāda* is this process of dependent co-arising or dependent co-origination, which conditions *dukkha*.

Two Methods

The way to benefit from this teaching is not to allow the dependent co-arising to take place. One method for doing this is to cut the process off right at the moment of sense contact. Do not allow the development of *vedanā*, do not allow feelings of satisfaction or dissatisfaction to arise. When there is no production of *vedanā*, there is no birth of the craving and clinging that is the "I" and "mine." The "I" and "mine" lie right there at the birth of craving and clinging; illusion lies right there. If *paṭicca-samuppāda* is stopped just there at the moment of sense contact, when there is nothing but sense contact, there is no way for the "I" and "mine" to arise. Then there is no spiritual disease and no *dukkha*.

If this first method is not possible, there is another method. For the average person, it is extremely difficult to prevent sense contact (*phassa*) from developing into *vedanā*. As soon as there is sense contact, the feelings of satisfaction or dissatisfaction always follow immediately. The process doesn't stop at *phassa* because most of us have never been trained in Dhamma. But there is still a way to save ourselves: when *vedanā* has already developed, although there is already a feeling of satisfaction or dissatisfaction, stop it right there. Let feeling remain merely as feeling and then pass away. Don't allow it to go on and concoct *taṇhā*, foolishly wanting this and that in reaction to the satisfaction and dissatisfaction. Once there is satisfaction, there is desire, craving, indulgence, possessiveness, envy, and their string of consequences. Once there is dissatisfaction, there is the desire to harm, to hurt, to devastate, and even to kill. If there are these sorts of desires in the mind, it means that *vedanā* has already concocted *taṇhā*. In this case, one must suffer from the spiritual disease of *dukkha*, and nobody can help. All the gods together cannot help. The Buddha said that even he cannot help. He has no power over the Law of Nature; he is merely the one who reveals it, so that others can practice in accordance with it. If one practices correctly, one doesn't suffer. Thus, it is said, if *vedanā* has concocted *taṇhā*, nobody can help. As soon as any form of craving has arisen, there inevitably must be *dukkha*.[42]

In that turbulent wanting that arises in the mind, see how to distinguish the feeling of the "desirer," of "I," of the self or ego, which wants this or wants that, which wants to do it like this or like that, which has acted in this way or that, or which has received the results of those actions. That one who desires is "I." Wanting things, it grasps them as "mine" in some way or another: "my" status, "my" property, "my" safety, "my" victory. In all of those feelings the "I" is also present.

The feeling of "I" and "mine" is called *upādāna* (attachment), which arises from *taṇhā* (craving). *Taṇhā* conditions *upādāna*. If *paṭicca-samuppāda* has progressed as far as *taṇhā* and *upādāna*, the germ that entered through the eye, ear, nose, tongue, or body has matured to the extent that it expresses itself as the symptoms of the disease, because *upādāna* is followed by existence (*bhava*). *Upādāna* conditions the arising of *bhava*. *Bhava* means "having and being." The having and being of what? The having and being of "I" and "mine." *Kammabhava* is the action (*kamma*) that conditions the arising of "I" and "mine." If it is called simply *bhava*, it means the state of "I" and "mine" full blown, the disease full blown.

JUST EXPERIENCING

In our practice we must stop the process right at the point where sense contact (*phassa*) conditions *vedanā*, or, if we fail there, we must prevent *vedanā* from concocting *taṇhā*. After that it's hopeless. We try to have Dhamma right there at the meeting of eye and forms, of ear and sounds, of tongue and flavors, and so on, by continually training in the fact that nothing whatsoever should be clung to. With ordinary people, once sense contact takes place, *vedanā* arises followed by *taṇhā*, *upādāna*, *bhava*, and *jāti* (birth). This is a path so well worn that it is extremely easy to follow.

Now, try not to take that path anymore. As soon as there is sense contact, turn around and take the path of mindfulness and wisdom. Don't take the path of "I" and "mine." Or, if you follow it as far as *vedanā*, try to turn back from there to the path of *sati-paññā*. Don't just float along with the stream of "I" and "mine." In this way, there is never any *dukkha*, neither day nor night. If we can practice skillfully, and perfectly follow the correct method to the end, we can realize Arahantship ourselves.

If we wish to go by the Buddha's words, there is an easy principle that the Buddha taught to a disciple named Bāhiya. "O Bāhiya, whenever you see a form, let there be just the seeing; whenever you hear a sound, let there be just the hearing; when you smell an odor, let there be just the smelling; when you taste a flavor, let there be just the tasting; when a thought arises, let it be just a natural phenomenon arising in the mind. When you practice like this, there will be no self, no "I". When there is no self, there will be no running that way and no coming this way and no stopping anywhere. Self doesn't exist. That is the end of *dukkha*. That itself is *nibbāna*."[43] Whenever life is like that, it's *nibbāna*. If it's lasting, then it's lasting *nibbāna*; if it's temporary, then it's temporary *nibbāna*. In other words, there is just one principle to live by.

Whatever method of practice you adopt, it should lead to equanimity or quenching regarding the sense objects that make contact. Whatever sort of insight meditation you do, if you do it correctly without deceiving yourself, it must take this one form, the identical form, that of not letting sense data be concocted into the feeling of "I" and "mine." Then it's not difficult to destroy defilements since, when you practice like this, they are destroyed as a matter of course.

To make a simple comparison, if we want to prevent rats from coming around and disturbing us, we keep a cat. All we have to do is look after the cat, and the rats will disappear without our having to catch them ourselves. The cat just goes about its business and there are no more rats. Because of the cat, the undesirable thing is no more.

LIVING RIGHTLY

If we merely oversee the eyes, ears, nose, tongue, body, and mind in the proper manner, the killing of defilements occurs naturally. This is to speak in conventional terms. It is the same as in the Buddha's teaching, "Bhikkhus, if you live rightly, the world will not be without Arahants" (*Ime ce bhikkhave bhikkhū sammā vihareyum asuñño loko Arahantehi assa*).[44] Pay close attention to this. Just live in the right way—you don't have to do anything more than that—and the world will not be void of Arahants. This is not a minor point.

Sammā vihareyyum means "to live rightly." How is it to live rightly so that the world will not be void of Arahants? To live rightly is to live untouched by forms, sounds, odors, flavors, and physical sensations. In other words, they are experienced, but they do not enter and concoct feeling (*vedanā*), craving (*tanhā*), and clinging (*upādāna*). Thus, we live intelligently. We live with mindfulness and wisdom, void of "I" and "mine," for we have studied enough and have practiced until we are sufficiently adept. So having made contact, the sense object dies like a wave breaking on the shore, just as if we have a cat in our house that kills the rats that enter from other houses or the forest.

If we live in the right way, according to the principles of nonclinging, forms, sounds, odors, flavors, and physical sensations cannot harm us. We experience them and associate with them but treat them with mindfulness and wisdom. Then we can eat them, consume them, possess them, or keep them without *dukkha* resulting, just as if they don't exist. The result is the same as if we don't use them, don't eat them, don't keep them, because there is no "us" or "ours."

On the other hand, when everything is done with "I" and "mine," there is *dukkha* all the time. Even before consuming or keeping, there is already *dukkha*, and while actually consuming or keeping there is further *dukkha*. The whole thing becomes miserable due to this cause. To be vexed with the disease of *dukkha* is called "not living rightly."

When we live rightly, there is no way for the disease to arise. If we live rightly, the defilements (*kilesa*) have no food to sustain them. They must starve and die. Starving the defilements can be compared to caging a fierce tiger in a pen where there is no food. We don't have to kill it; it will die of its own accord. In the same way, we encircle and trap forms, sounds, odors, flavors, physical sensations, and mental phenomena right at the point where they contact the eyes, ears, nose, tongue, body, and mind. We cage them right there. If we practice correctly toward those things right there at the very point of contact, the defilements have no way to get food. The tiger of defilement starves to death. In other words, the germ of defilement can no longer breed further defilement or cause *dukkha*.

The Buddha taught that if we live rightly—simply live in the correct way—the earth will not be void of Arahants. This is called practicing according to the principle of *paṭicca-samuppāda* (dependent co-origination). It is the kind of right living by which defilements cannot arise, because we see that "I" and "mine" are mere illusions that only arise when sense contact gives rise to feeling, which then concocts craving. If the concocting of craving is avoided, clinging to "I" and "mine" does not take place.

You should understand correctly that "I" and "mine" is a product of concoction; it's not real. It's an illusion in the same way that a wave arising from blowing wind is an illusion. The water is real and the wind is real, but the wave is an illusion. Here we use a material phenomenon for the sake of comparison, and the comparison is not perfect. We merely mean to indicate the illusoriness of a wave that arises due to concocting: the wind blows across the water, a ridge of water arises, and then it disappears. The feeling of "I" and "mine," which arises over and over in a day, is like a wave. The water of the sense experience is contacted by the wind of delusion or ignorance, and waves of "I" and "mine" are formed over and over again throughout the day.

SPIRITUAL BIRTH

A single emergence of the feeling of "I" and "mine" is called one birth (*jāti*). This is the real meaning of the word "birth." Don't take it to mean birth from a mother's womb. A person is born from the womb once and gets laid out in the coffin once. That's not the birth the Buddha pointed to; that's much too physical. The Buddha was pointing to a spiritual birth, the birth of clinging to "I" and "mine." In one day there can be hundreds of such births. The number depends on a person's facility for it, but in each birth the "I" and "mine" arises, slowly fades, gradually disappears, and dies. Shortly, on contact with another sense object, "I" and "mine" arise again.

Each "birth" generates a reaction that carries over to the next. This is what is called "the old *kamma* of a previous birth ripening in the present birth," which is then transmitted further. Every birth carries on the process. This is how to understand the "fruit of action" (*kamma-vipāka*) and the reception of *kamma's* results. Such an interpretation agrees with the Buddha's own words; any other interpretation strays from the point. We must understand birth, *kamma*, and the fruits of *kamma* in the correct way. For example, there can be birth as the desirer of some pleasing object, and then death followed by birth as a thief, and then a further death followed by birth as the enjoyer of that object. In a short time, there is birth as a prisoner in the dock. Then, guilt having been established, birth occurs as a convict in jail. These sorts of birth are many and muddled; they are like a multitude of threads tangled together. If you look closely, however, you will understand that if one stops birth, then at that moment there is *nibbāna*—that which is not born, does not age, does not sicken, and does not die. If there is still birth, still the feeling of "I" and "mine," the wheel of birth and death keeps turning as a continual cycle of *dukkha*.

We shouldn't think, however, that absence of birth means that one is so empty that there is no feeling at all. It does not mean sitting stiffly like a log of wood. On the contrary, one is extremely active. Being perfectly void of birth, void of "I," is to have perfect mindfulness and wisdom. Whatever one does is completely fluent. There being no false thinking, false speech, or false action, one acts swiftly and surely. There is no possibility of error because one's *sati-paññā* is natural and spontaneous. This state of mind is called "void of I." The person who is void of "I," who is *nibbāna*, can do anything and do it without error. Her or his actions are many, are extremely swift, and are greatly beneficial.

Don't think that this sort of experience makes you unable to do anything, that you'll just stop everything and be lethargic, weary, and indifferent. That's your own idea. Your foolishness makes you afraid of *suññatā*, afraid of *nibbāna*, afraid that ending your craving will be unpleasant.

In fact, the ending of craving is the ultimate pleasure and the greatest happiness. It is true pleasure and happiness. It is not harmful, deceitful, or illusory. The pleasure of the ordinary unenlightened person is false; it is deceitful, is illusory, and fills one with *dukkha*. It is like bait, which catches us on its hook when we swallow it. Ordinary enjoyment of pleasure is called "falling into the hands of the devil." In such a state there is unceasing confusion. One is trapped on the wheel of birth and death, in the chain or the whirlpool of *dukkha*, unable to get free.

11. *Sensory Illusions*

S EEING THE "I" AND "MINE" as an illusion by practicing the principle of dependent co-origination (*paṭicca-samuppāda*) is one path to understanding *suññatā*. Now we will consider another method: seeing that even the sense objects—forms, sounds, odors, flavors, tangible objects, and mental phenomena—are illusion. This second method involves an understanding of impermanence, unsatisfactoriness, and not-self (*aniccatā, dukkhatā,* and *anattatā*).

IMPERMANENCE, UNSATISFACTORINESS, AND NOT-SELF

We must not take the subjects of impermanence, unsatisfactoriness, and selflessness lightly. They are not just issues for old people nor merely words to be chanted when someone dies. They are subjects that we all must take up and use in our everyday lives. Anyone capable of using their understanding of impermanence, unsatisfactoriness, and selflessness to manage their daily life possesses the ultimate antibody. For such a person, forms, sounds, odors, flavors, and so on cannot turn into poison. Such a one has security (*khema*). Notice that the Buddha didn't use the word "happy," because that word can sometimes be misleading, or even deceptive. "Secure" is good enough. It means free and peaceful.

We should be clear about the meaning of *khema*. It means "secure from the disturbances (*yogas*)."[45] To be secure from the things that disturb us is to be void, which is *nibbāna*. If you want a secure life, you must rely on a thorough understanding of impermanence, suffering, and not-self. Then you can withstand the forms, sounds, odors, flavors, and physical sensations that you experience without getting lost in aversion or attraction. There are just two kinds of confusion: getting lost in attraction and getting lost in aversion. One causes laughter and the other causes tears. If one sees that laughter is just one form of panting, gasping, and weariness, and that crying is just another—and if one sees that to remain even minded is better—such knowledge is security. We don't become the slaves of sense objects, laughing and crying according to their enticements. We are free, at rest, secure. To use impermanence, unsatisfactoriness, and selflessness as a tool to govern our daily lives is better than lolling in confusion. We will be able to see that the sense objects are illusions. Just as we see "I" and "mine" as illusion because they are conditioned by sense objects, so we see the sense objects themselves as illusory through the principle of impermanence, unsatisfactoriness, and soullessness. In this way, the disease of *dukkha* does not break out.

PLEASANT FEELINGS

Yet a third method of contacting *suññatā* is to examine *sukhavedanā*, that is, pleasure, enjoyment, and delight. Pleasant feeling (*sukhavedanā*) is an illusion because it's like a wave that only arises periodically; there's no reality to it. I am making this point because every single thing in every single world is valued according to the positive feelings it provides. Really think about this. Why are you studying? Why are you doing the job that you do? Why do you amass wealth and status, fame and followers? Solely for the sake of pleasant feelings! If we understand just this one matter and deal with it correctly, everything will come right. So we must see positive feeling in its true light, as one form of illusion.

We must deal with happiness or pleasant feeling (*sukhavedanā*) in accordance with its illusory nature. To develop an aversion toward it would be foolish, as would be getting infatuated with it and becoming its slave. To deal with it correctly is Dhamma, is to be a disciple of the Buddha, for one can defeat *dukkha* and avoid suffering the spiritual disease. We deal with positive feeling by the method of contemplating its illusory nature, seeing that it's like a wave that arises due to wind blowing across water. In other words, when forms, sounds, odors, and flavors approach, the foolishness of ignorance and delusion goes out to receive them. From that contact, the wave of pleasant feeling arises and then breaks up and disintegrates. If we look at it like this, we won't be its slave. We will be capable of dealing with pleasure in a way that is free from *dukkha*. Our family will be without *dukkha*, our neighbors will be without *dukkha*, and the whole world will be without *dukkha*—and we will be the root cause. If everyone understood positive feeling (*sukha-vedanā*) and was free of *dukkha*, the world would have lasting peace and true, enduring happiness. This is the benefit of recovering from spiritual disease through these various methods: one does not suffer from the disease of "I" or the disease of "mine."

Let's review the first set of three practice methods, and then sum up the essential perspective on practicing with *suññatā*. We can see the illusoriness of "I" and "mine" through the principle of dependent co-origination (*paṭicca-samuppāda*); the illusoriness of the six kinds of sense objects through the principle of impermanence, unsatisfactoriness, and selflessness (*aniccatā*, *dukkhatā*, and *anattatā*); and the illusoriness of pleasant feeling (*sukhavedanā*) through its wave-like nature. For any of these practice methods to be effective, we must look closely, be attentive, and have plenty of mindfulness and wisdom at the moment that sense objects come into contact by way of eye, ear, nose, tongue, body, and mind. As the Buddha enjoined the Venerable Bāhiya: let seeing be merely seeing and hearing be merely hearing. Don't concoct *vedanā* or, if *vedanā* has already developed, don't let that concoct *taṇhā*.

12. Practicing at "Ordinary Times"

I T'S IMPORTANT TO UNDERSTAND various methods of practice, but these methods also must be explained together with the opportunities and occasions for practice. We will consider three occasions or times for practice:

the "ordinary times";
the moments of sense contact through the six sense doors;
and the moment of physical death, when the mind "goes out."

How should we practice on the first occasion, at times when there is no particular association with sense objects? These "ordinary times" occur when we are doing some kind of work alone and unconcerned. Perhaps we are performing our daily tasks, practicing some kind of formal meditation, reading a book in our spare time, or even thinking about something; yet the mind is undisturbed by sense contact. At such times, our practice must be the study and realization of how things are void. When there are no problems due to sense contact, how is the mind void, how is it not deluded by everything? Think about it, study it for yourself, ask others about it, and discuss it regularly. Keep working on it continuously.

NOT WORTH HAVING

There is another way to practice that is particularly suited to laypeople, people who have never been ordained or have never studied the scriptures. It's straightforward enough even for those who cannot read at all. However, its aim is the same as that of other methods: to know the *suññatā* of all things. The method is to observe whether there is anything worth having or being. Ordinary people ought to live examining whether anything is worth having, getting, or being. "Having and getting" refers to getting silver and gold, gaining wealth, gaining possessions, getting prestige, and getting power. What is worth having or worth getting? Being a human being, being an animal, being a millionaire, being a beggar, being a king, being a citizen, being a celestial being—what sort of being is worth being?

First, we must understand the words "to have," "to get," and "to be" correctly. These words directly refer to grasping and clinging. There must be grasping at something, if we are to take it as "ours," in order to fulfill the meaning of the words "having" and "getting." For instance, suppose we pile up diamonds and jewels so they fill a room, but there is no clinging to them, no feeling of "I got" or "I am the owner." It would be the same as if there were no having or getting. The pile of precious stones would sit there without any meaning. But if the feeling of grasping at "I" occurs, the feeling that "I have got them" or "I have made them mine," then this would constitute "having" or "getting." Please understand these words in this way.

I'll ask again, what is there worth having? What is there worth gaining? What is there to have that won't cause its owner suffering? Every single existing thing will burn up its owner; will pierce, strangle, and entangle him; will dominate and oppress him should he start to have or to be. But should the precious stones be piled up while he has no feeling of having or being, then there would be no burning, entangling, or strangling of any kind. This is called "not-having" and "not-being." So what is there that won't be *dukkha* once it is become or gotten?

Once there is the feeling of having or being, we don't have to be in the room with these jewels; we can be in the forest or in another country on the other side of the world, and the mind will still experience *dukkha*. Try having children grow up and live in a foreign country. You'll see that if you still cling to "I" and "mine," they will be able to give you sleepless nights, or even a nervous breakdown, in spite of the fact that they're far away. That's the exact meaning of "having" and "being."

DOER-LESS DOING

Please make it a habit to regularly contemplate what is worth having and what is worth being. What is there that, once possessed or become, will not cause *dukkha*? When we discover the truth that there is absolutely nothing worthy of the feelings of having and being, we become even-minded toward all things. Whatever action we perform, be it arranging, having, collecting, using, or whatever, we just do what needs to be done. So don't let the mind have or become! Don't feel the sense of "I get," "I am," or "I have." Keep in mind the Dhamma principle of doer-less doing:

> The doing is done, but no doer can be found.
> The path has been walked to its end, but no walker is there.[46]

This verse refers to the Arahant, the one who has practiced Dhamma, who has walked the Noble Path to its very end and reached *nibbāna* with no walker or practitioner to be found.

The principle of doer-less doing must be taken up and utilized in our daily lives. Whether we're eating, sitting, lying down, standing, walking, consuming, using, seeking, or whatever, we must have enough *sati-paññā* to prevent the feelings of "I am": "the doer," "the eater," "the walker," "the sitter," "the sleeper," "the user." This keeps the mind constantly void of ego, so that *suññatā* is the natural state, and we live with the awareness that there is nothing worth having or being.

Dhamma can be practiced in conjunction with our daily tasks and the movements they entail, and this is an extremely high level of Dhamma practice. There is no need to separate Dhamma from everyday life. Just have this mindfulness and ready wisdom (*sati-sampajañña*)[47] of doer-less doing. Not only will the work be successful and free from error, but at the same time the Dhamma will develop and grow exceedingly. Doer-less doing is to live naturally and ordinarily in not-having and not-gaining.

NOT WORTH BEING

"Being" is even easier. Consider what one might be that wouldn't be *dukkha*. This can be a formula for reflection; it is an essential point. "What is there to be that won't be *dukkha*?" The word "being," just as with the words "having" and "gaining," refers only to the being that is accompanied by *upādāna*: being that includes grasping and clinging to "I am." For example, if a room is piled full of gold, but we don't feel we're the owner, there is no gaining or having, and no being. Although legal ownership rights and worldly social conventions have a certain validity, in our true hearts we shouldn't be misled into taking those relative truths as absolute. For instance, when a person gives birth to a child, it is natural that the one who gives birth is the mother and the one born is the child. However, if one doesn't attach to being mother, one won't be a mother. Because one delusively presumes oneself to be a mother, one becomes one.

We should regard this as an animal instinct. Animals feel like mother chickens, mother dogs, or mother cows. They feel themselves to be mothers and naturally love their young. They needn't create, force, or nurture such feelings. These are instincts natural to animals. To reach the level of mindfulness and wisdom, one must do better than that. One must know how to destroy the grasping and clinging that arises from such ignorance.

Now, some people will think, "How cruel and heartless, not to let us feel ourselves to be mothers! Won't you let us love our children?" Please listen carefully. That isn't the meaning at all. It's possible to be a mother and perform a mother's duties with *sati-paññā*. It's not necessary to act with desire and attachment, which bring on every kind of *dukkha*.

94

With *dukkha* tears will flow, the heart will be dry and anxious, and there won't be any joy. That suffering is indeed the price of not knowing how to be a mother, of being a mother in a way that does not conform with Dhamma. Such is the *dukkha* of "mothers."

When one is a mother, one must have the *dukkha* of a mother; when one is a child, one must have the *dukkha* of a child; when one is a father, one must have the *dukkha* of a father. Try asking yourself, "Is being their mother a pleasure?" "Is being their father any fun?" Those of you old enough to have had a full experience of parenthood, think over what it's like. How will you answer? Even if you don't say anything outright, probably every one of you will shake your heads. Is being a mother any fun? Is being a father a pleasure? This is something that you should study. Regularly and naturally be conscious of it at the times when the mind is not occupied with sense contact.

Is it a pleasure being a husband? Is it fun being a wife? Think it over for yourselves. Those who have fully experienced what it is to be husbands and wives will all shake their heads.

Is it enjoyable being female? Is it a pleasure being male? If your mindfulness and wisdom is developing step by step and becoming increasingly refined, you will all shake your heads. To be female is to have the *dukkha* of a female. To be male is to have the *dukkha* of a male.

Is it enjoyable being a child? Is it fun being an adult? Young children will probably say, "Yes, it's fun." We who are now adults, who are now old enough, should look back and ask ourselves, "Was it really a pleasure?" Children have the *dukkha* of children and adults have the *dukkha* of adults, as long as there is grasping and clinging.

To be anything that has an opposite, or to be nothing at all—which is better? To be an ordinary person, to be a denizen of hell—are they worth it? Is being a human worth it? Is being an animal worth it? Is it worth being this person who you are? Or is it worth being a celestial being (*deva*)[48] in heaven? These questions provide measures of a person's mindfulness and wisdom, of whether or not one sees grasping and clinging fully and rightly. Those who have thoroughly seen the painful consequences of grasping and clinging will shake their heads in the same way, because being a person one must have the *dukkha* of a person, and being a *deva* one must have the *dukkha* of a *deva*. If we are void, not taking ourselves to be anything at all, then we are neither a person nor a *deva*, and the respective *dukkha* of each is absent. If one is a human being or a deva following the urgings of grasping and clinging, is it a pleasure? Those who have realized the truth will all shake their heads.

FOOLED AGAIN

To bring it in more closely, is it worth being a good person? Is it worth being a bad person? If we ask who wants to be a good person, there is likely to be a forest of raised hands. Such people don't yet see that attachment to being a good person means one must have the good person's sort of *dukkha* in exactly the same way that a bad person will have the *dukkha* appropriate to a bad person. When there is grasping and clinging at being, then there is no happiness at all. This is due to one sort of heaviness or another, which is intrinsic to that state of being itself. Some kinds of *dukkha* do not show themselves openly, because of pleasures or distractions that cover them up. Nevertheless, because we are fooled by those pleasures and distractions, we must endure the *dukkha* of having, being, and gaining, the *dukkha* of ambitiously or excitedly striving to be this and that.

In truth, nature fools us into taking on *dukkha*. An obvious example is the *dukkha* that arises from propagating the species and from giving birth. It fools us so much that people actually volunteer enthusiastically for such labor. If they were to see the truth for themselves, they would never play with these deceptions of nature. Is it fun being a good person? Is it pleasant being a bad person? Think about it.

Coming even closer, is it worth being a fortunate person? Is it worth being an unfortunate person? The hasty and uncircumspect are likely to raise their hands immediately, claiming that being fortunate is extremely pleasant. But those who have fully experienced good fortune will shake their heads. One who is fortunate must endure the *dukkha* of one who attaches to being fortunate, in exactly the same way that the one who is unfortunate must endure the *dukkha* appropriate to one who cannot bear to be unfortunate.

BEING HAPPY

Coming closer still, is it worth being a happy person? Is it worth being an unhappy person? There will be a forest of raised hands here, all asking to be happy people. On the other hand, those who have been happy, who have fully experienced the happiness others are clamoring for, will shake their heads. They know that the happy person endures the *dukkha* of happiness. You may not understand this point, so let me repeat: people who are happy must experience the *dukkha* of happy people. You must notice that worldlings assume, establish, and attach to the conventions concerning the nature of happiness. One who has money, power, influence, wealth, all the sensual pleasures, and other such things is a happy person. But if we look closely, we will see that there is kind of *dukkha* appropriate to happy people. These kinds of happiness have hidden "fish bones" in them.

Even with the more subtle forms of happiness that arise from concentration (*samādhi*), the meditative "attainments" (*samāpatti*), and the meditative absorptions (*jhānas*), if the feeling that "I am happy" arises, then it too will form a "fish bone" in the flesh of that happiness and will stick in one's throat. Those who grasp at and cling to the happiness of the *jhānas* and attainments suffer accordingly.

Consequently, there is the teaching of renouncing lust for form (*rūpa-rāga*) and lust for the formless (*arūpa-rāga*), which are the first two of the higher fetters (*saṁyojana*) that prevent people from being Arahants. If there is clinging to the idea that we have happiness, even if it's the happiness that arises from Dhamma, there will still be a refined kind of "fish bone" sticking in the throat, and the true Dhamma cannot be discerned.

Grasping at *nibbāna* as being "my self" or "my happiness" is impossible. One may say, if one wishes, that *nibbāna* is the supreme happiness, and then attach to *nibbāna* as being "I" or "mine." One may say, "I have the happiness of *nibbāna*" or "I have attained *nibbāna*." But these are mere verbalizations. In fact, one who still grasps and clings cannot possibly realize *nibbāna*. If anyone takes himself to be the enjoyer of *nibbāna's* happiness, that can only be a counterfeit *nibbāna*. True *nibbāna* is not of a nature that can be grasped at in this way.

So we pursue many types of happiness—from that of children, through the happiness of youth, of adults, of the elderly, of the powerful and influential, on up through the happiness of being a *deva*, of having meditative absorptions and attainments—until we reach whatever we believe to be the highest happiness. If we ever delusively consider that "I am happy," we must suffer accordingly. Those who have realized the truth see this fact. Those who have not are in turmoil, ambitiously and hungrily striving for wealth, power, and sense pleasures. Or, on a higher level, they are greedily striving for insight, meditative absorptions, and attainments. Some push so hard they end up in mental hospitals. That in itself demonstrates the danger of grasping and clinging to happiness. Young children will not understand this point, but those advanced in years should.

BIRTH AND DEATH

Now we'll give some thought to another pair of opposites. Is being born a pleasure? Is dying a pleasure? Choose one or the other. Which is more fun, being born or dying? Which is more worthwhile, being a born person or being a dead person? If we really understand Dhamma we'll shake our heads; we'll want neither birth nor death. However, ordinary people don't want to die. They only want to be born. They want birth without death and, what's more, they want eternal life. Or, if they must die, they want to be reborn. This indeed is grasping and clinging. In short, the person born suffers one way and the person dying suffers another way. Only when there is neither birth nor death, when there is *suññatā*, will there be an end to *dukkha*.

Why not amuse yourself by thinking this over when you're lying down, sitting, or walking, in the moments when no sense object has made contact? Or, when you're doing something or being something, why not try thinking in the way we have described?

When you're weary, exhausted, and distressed with being a mother, father, or something else, why don't you ever feel that it isn't much fun? Being a husband, being a wife, being any of the things that I've mentioned—when you're disturbed and upset by that state of being, why don't you ever feel it to be utterly unpleasant? You still find it enjoyable even when it brings you to tears.

There is a final pair to consider—birth and non-birth. We must reflect and investigate carefully that both birth and non-birth are too much trouble, for neither is void and free. If we cling to not being born, this clinging too is not void (*suñña*). This part, concerning birth and non-birth, the final pair, is the hardest to understand and the hardest to practice. We must want neither birth nor non-birth. Through not grasping at or clinging to either of them, there is voidness. Having spoken continually about having and being, of not-having and not-being, we come to birth and non-birth. Almost immediately, we grasp at non-birth. Thus, at the final stage, our practice must advance to the point where our knowledge of non-birth dissolves without becoming an object of grasping and clinging. Then there appears true *suññatā*, in which there is neither birth nor non-birth, in other words, true non-birth, the remainderless quenching.

This manner of speaking may seem to be quibbling or wrestling back and forth, but the meaning is unequivocal. There is a definite difference between true and false non-birth. So don't cling to the idea that *nibbāna* is non-birth and is wonderful and amazing in this way and that. And don't attach to the cycles of birth and death (*vaṭṭasaṁsāra*) as a plethora of fun-filled births. There must be no grasping at or clinging to either side for there to be *suññatā* and genuine non-birth. The practice during ordinary times must continually be of this nature.

A special mention should be made of the higher work of meditation (*kammaṭṭhāna*), mental development through the power of concentration

99

(*samādhi-bhāvanā*), or contemplation leading to insight (*vipassanā*). These three terms refer to systematic techniques for understanding the painful consequences of grasping and clinging. Yet these practices still fall under the category of "ordinary times," especially in the sense that all practice comes down to being void of attachment. If we still cling to the "meditator," it isn't really meditation yet. In proper meditation, however, the mind isn't disturbed by sense objects. So don't let yourself be born as a "meditator"; instead, see the voidness of meditation.

13. Practicing at the Moment of Contact and the Moment of Death

W E'VE DISCUSSED THE FIRST OCCASION for practice: the "ordinary times." The second occasion for practice is the moment when sense objects make contact. When visible forms, sounds, odors, flavors, and tangible objects contact the eyes, ears, nose, tongue, and body, we must practice letting contact (*phassa*) stop at contact, letting *vedanā* (feeling) stop at *vedanā*, and so on. Letting contact stop just at contact is the most excellent level of practice. On a more ordinary level, contact develops into *vedanā*, but we stop it right there, without allowing any further development into craving and grasping at "I" and "mine." We considered this method earlier when we discussed the contemplation of dependent co-origination.

Some of the preachers and teachers in monastery halls and Buddhist colleges say that stopping right at contact (*phassa*) is impossible, that *vedanā* (feeling) always develops. Such people cling to their books, to the literal meaning of words, or to certain examples, rather than the truth.

In fact, the Buddha taught that when seeing forms just see, when smelling odors just smell, when tasting flavors just taste, and when touching tangible objects just touch. If you can do it, then there is no you. The ego is not born. This is the end of *dukkha*; this is continuous voidness.

101

Just observe your own reactions at the times when you glance in the direction of some neutral form. Try casting your eyes on the door or a window and you'll notice that there is merely contact; there are no feelings of satisfaction or dissatisfaction. When visible forms, sounds, odors, flavors, and tangible objects enter as contact, let them stop right there without any satisfaction or dissatisfaction occurring.

Be like the soldier asleep next to a large cannon. When a shell is fired, he merely registers the sound without feeling anything and just goes on sleeping happily. No matter how heavy the shelling, he is not startled or disturbed. There is just the sound of the cannon contacting his ear and then ceasing.

When you hear the sound of a man, of a woman, or of a lover, can you let contact stop at contact in that same way? If you can, then you're really adept. Here animals may be more accomplished than people, because they lack all the excess mental baggage we carry. If we wish to reach that peak of excellence, we must train ourselves to let *phassa* remain as merely *phassa*.

If you can't do it and concede defeat, you can still stop at *vedanā*. As soon as there is a feeling of comfort or discomfort, of satisfaction or dissatisfaction, then quench it just there, without giving birth to the various kinds of desire that spring from the urges of defilement, craving, and attachment. This is how to practice on the occasion of contact with sense objects.

The Last Chance

The third occasion for practice is the moment when the mind quenches. The body will break up and die; how can we practice *suññatā* at that time? In this situation, we must depend on having taken "remainderless quenching" as our basic principle throughout life.

The natural death of the aged is something definite and sure. When someone reaches old age, it's said that one has little time left. What can be achieved in that short remaining time? To avoid running out of time, those who are old and unlearned, who don't have the time to study very much and whose brains aren't as good as they once were, can hold to the principle of the remainderless quenching of the "I," which we have been discussing.

Regularly contemplate that being a person is no fun, being a *deva* (celestial being) is no fun, being a father is not pleasant, being a mother is not pleasant. Being a son, a daughter, a husband, a wife, a servant, a master, a victor, a loser, a good person, a bad person, a fortunate person, or an unfortunate person is unpleasant. None of them are pleasant, none of them are any fun. Then the mind will hold no hope of having or being anything at all. One could say, "all hope has been given up."

This phrase "given up hope" may also be used in regard to the attainment of Arahantship. But it doesn't mean the resignation of the foolish and lazy; it's a different matter altogether. It is the hopelessness of one who has true wisdom, who sees that there is nothing in this or any world that one should wish to have or be. Truly, nothing is worth having or being, at any time or in any place.

What path will be taken by the mind of the "hopeless person"? It won't take any path at all, because it sees that nothing anywhere is worth wishing for. Thus, this mind tends toward its own dissolution. There being no desire to have or be anything, it dissolves into *suññatā*. This is the skillful means to cheat nature a little. When the time has really come for the mind to cease, revive the feeling that nothing anywhere is worth having or being. If that feeling is present in the mind at the moment it ceases, it will reach *nibbāna* inevitably. Have the body and mind cease with the feeling that nothing is worth having or being, then it will realize *nibbāna* in that physical death itself. What a deal: making such a tiny investment, yet certain of the best results!

Let the greatest scholars of the land come to test what it's like for the mind to meet death with the authentic feeling that nothing anywhere is worth having or being. It will be the kind of dissolution that dissolves by *nibbāna-dhātu* (coolness element). It will be *nibbāna-dhātu* in itself. Anyone, no matter how unlearned and inarticulate, who experiences just this single thing will find it sufficient.

When the time of death has truly come, let this feeling be present. You should remember that when close to death the mind will gradually slip away. As the body runs down near its end, awareness will gradually disappear. You will forget more and more until you forget everything. You won't know what time it is, whether it's day or night; you won't be able to tell where you are or whose house you're in; you won't even be able to remember your name. But the awareness that nothing is worth having or being can stay on as the mind's companion to the very end. Volunteer for the remainderless quenching! Keep that feeling of volunteering for remainderless quenching, including the readiness to accept it, as the mind's partner until the very end. With this skillful means, the mind will be able to dissolve itself into the *suññatā* that is *nibbāna*. This is how people of little knowledge must practice at the moment of physical death. With this trick, an unlearned grandma or granddad can quench perfectly. We call it the trick of turning a fall from a ladder into a calculated leap.

THE ART OF LEAPING

The body must inevitably break up; it's old and has reached its end. In other words, you are about to fall from the ladder. As you fall you must leap. Leap into the remainderless quenching by experiencing in the mind that nothing is worth having or being. This may be called leaping in the right direction. In this leap, there is no pain of any sort. On the contrary, there is the best possible result—attainment of remainderless quenching. This is how to leap like a master, to really know how to fall from the ladder.

Please don't fall like the fools who break their necks and all their limbs. Even those who have studied a lot and travel about giving fancy talks in monastery halls can still fall from the ladder and break all their bones. They can't compare with those who have been interested in the right way, even if only in this one matter, and can thereby save their skins.

What is one to do in the event of accidental death, such as getting run over by a car, having a building collapse on top of one, being gored from the rear by a bull, or getting blown up by a nuclear bomb? If you have a little intelligence, you'll see that it's exactly the same. If there is even a tiny amount of awareness left, in that moment, you must resolve on the remainderless quenching. Through having previously developed the feeling that there is nothing worth having or being until it is completely fluent and natural, you will be able to bring it to mind for that split second before the end. Someone run over by a car doesn't die immediately. There is always an interval, if only a fraction of a second or a single thought moment. For the flash of awareness that resolves on remainderless quenching, that is plenty of time.

What if death occurs too suddenly, without any awareness? That itself is the remainderless quenching, because we have already trained in ordinary moments to keep this awareness, that nothing is worth having or being, constantly in the mind. As I have already explained, when nothing special is happening, train your awareness until the mind is always inclining toward remainderless quenching. Even when the body meets death with no opportunity to think or feel anything, if this awareness has been continually present, there will be remainderless quenching. And if there is half a second, even one thought moment, we can think comfortably. So don't be cowardly, don't be afraid! Don't let cowardice and fear get in the way, crying, "please get me a doctor" or "take me to the hospital." If you go, you'll die there just the same. Why waste your remaining time?

People call it "unnatural death" when someone doesn't want to die and dies unexpectedly, even violently. The sublime Dhamma not only protects absolutely against unnatural death, it also brings one to *nibbāna* right there under the wheels of the car, beneath the collapsing building, at the horns of the bull, or in the pile of bodies charred by the nuclear blast. In place of a violent unnatural death, there is *nibbāna*.

Those who have studied little and don't know much are perfectly capable of understanding this teaching. They all should train in it, so they can leap from the ladder at the moment of death. As for the

105

death of those who have perfect knowledge and true mindfulness and wisdom; as for the death of those who have studied sufficiently and are proficient both in the theory and practice of Dhamma: for such people there's no need to leap as they fall from the ladder. They have been deathless since long before any physical illness began. Having long before attained a high level of Dhamma, for them there is no death.

For a person of such abundant knowledge, when the time of death truly arrives, his or her preparations will be much better than those of people who must leap as they fall from the ladder. Knowing how to establish incorruptible mindfulness and self-awareness (*sati-sampajañña*), one may laugh contemptuously at death. We can say that the wise descend the ladder smoothly. Because they don't fall, they needn't jump. So it is for those with perfect knowledge. Those who don't know so much had better be clever at leaping while falling from the ladder. This is the practice for being void in the final second.

Ready for Death

Now I would like to talk about the way that the diseased and dying should prepare themselves for death. When one knows that death is inevitable, such as when suffering from a terminal disease like tuberculosis or cancer, one should make the very best of it with *sati-sampajañña*, free of cowardice and fear.

I'd like to relate to you an account I once came across of the way people in the Buddha's time prepared for death. For those who regularly kept the precepts and religious practices, fasting was not at all difficult, because they were used to abstaining from the evening meal on *uposatha*[49] days. When their illness reached the point at which they felt they had no more than ten days left to live, they would stop eating. Not like us. These days, if someone is close to death, we go out and look for the most expensive and delicious foods, so that some people even die from the food. Back then, they avoided food in order to have a completely undisturbed mind. When the body starts to run down, it loses its ability to digest food, so that anything consumed turns to poison, which makes the mind restless and confused.

106

So they prepared themselves for death by abstaining from food and taking only water and medicine. As death came nearer, they would stop taking even water or medicine in order to focus their mindfulness and self-awareness and thus die in the way of remainderless quenching.

People who cling to goodness and virtue prepare themselves for death by clinging to goodness and virtue. The wise prepare themselves instead to let go and meet remainderless quenching. There is nothing that they want; injecting drugs to extend their lives would be a great irritation. This letting go is the meaning of "relinquishing the body" (*saṅkhāra*). Relinquishing the body while still alive, they prepare to make the best of its disintegration as the mind inclines toward remainderless quenching.

We who live in these modern times mill and mob around the doctor in a tumult, sometimes until the room is packed tight, trying to give the dying person more medicine, food, or injections. We try to do so many things that the sick person becomes anxious and flustered, and has no peace of mind. He doesn't know how he is going to die or whether in fact he will die at all. There is nothing but doubt and anxiety. The sick person does not experience victory over death, nor does he realize *suññatā* and the remainderless quenching about which we have been speaking.

Unlike the people of the Buddha's time, people today usually look for the most comfortable bed, the most comfortable room, the most expensive foods and medicines, and then die with a great fuss. We want to go on living, to put off death as long as possible, even if only for a single minute. We demand all sorts of injections and treatments, thus dying without any mindfulness and self-awareness. Such activity is deluded.

To die in the right way, we must have the daring of Dhamma and die victorious over death. To die as we have described is to realize *suññatā* in the last second of life. Please take care to remember that we still have a chance, right up to the last moment. If we are unable to beat death now or subsequently, in the final moment we can still be victorious.

These then are the ways to practice *suññatā*. We can contemplate

107

dependent co-origination; we can observe impermanence, unsatisfactoriness, and not-self in all things; and we can see the illusoriness of feelings. We apply our practice in "ordinary times," during moments of sense contact, and at the moment of death.

These are topics that should be brought up for thought, consultation, and regular discussion in the same way that we chat about radio and television programs, about politics, economics, and the general goings-on of the world. People who like boxing can get so excited about it that they can't get the words out quickly enough. Why can we talk about politics and sports all day and all night, yet when it comes to something as important as victory over death itself, we never discuss it at all?

Why don't we ever talk about fighting with death, about conquering death and being free of both birth and death? If we did, life would become easier straight away. If we discuss these things as much as we talk about other matters, in no time at all the practice of *suññatā* will become easy, like a hobby. When we follow the correct method, nothing is difficult and everything is easy, even the realization of *nibbāna*, leaping as we fall from the ladder.

14. Deliverance

YOU MUST NOW GO and observe yourself until you can grasp that, in fact, you yourself are frequently void. There are many times when you are unconfused and there is a great deal of mindfulness and wisdom. Disturbance, the feeling of "I" and "mine," comes every now and again. Its periodic and temporary arising is called "birth." Whenever there is birth, there is *dukkha*. But there are also many moments when there is no birth and so no *dukkha* at all. However, people stupidly skip over such moments, overlook the spontaneous *nibbāna*, and so are unaware of its presence.

WATCH YOURSELF

Even if it is only a very small *nibbāna*, merely a taste, it's exactly the same thing as true and lasting *nibbāna*. It differs only in duration. It doesn't last because we don't know how to protect ourselves from and destroy the spiritual disease. Consequently, every now and again the disease penetrates and interrupts *nibbāna*.

If one has been blessed with the intelligence to know that the mind is fundamentally void, that it's already *nibbāna*, then one only needs to be careful not to let it be infiltrated by new things. So don't let them in. Drive them out! If we don't let the germs of defilement into our house, we can be void all the time.

The way of driving out disease is to practice Dhamma according to the Buddha's teaching. This causes the arising of energy and inspiration: firm confidence in Dhamma (*chanda*), sincere effort in Dhamma (*viriya*), attention to Dhamma (*citta*), and unceasing alertness (*vimaṁsā*). With these four roads to success (*iddhipāda*) one will succeed without difficulty. If we start off foolishly, it's extremely difficult, harder than rolling a heavy mortar up a mountain; but if we approach practice in the right way, it's easier than rolling a mortar down a mountain.

The mind must also have unceasing self-awareness. Don't be forgetful and don't be heedless. Keep observing the voidness and busyness that arise daily. Let the mind love and be satisfied with *suññatā*, the ever-present *nibbāna*. Don't let it incline into wrong understanding and get lost in busy things.

Right now, the greatest problem is that nobody wants to end *dukkha*. People don't dare affirm that we are born in order to be free from *dukkha*. It has become as if we are born for anything at all, just so long as it's to our liking and good fun. We just blindly follow whatever's going. Actually, the ending of *dukkha* is not difficult. It's not beyond our capabilities, any more than any other job or work. But we don't understand, we turn our backs on freedom, and so we suffer.

THE BEST OF HEALTH

The ending of spiritual disease lies in knowing how to prevent the arising of "I" and "mine." Freedom from disease is called the greatest gain: the medicine sellers of the Buddha's time used to say, "Health is the greatest gain" (*Arogayā paramā lābhā*). They called out this phrase as they traveled along the highways: "Freedom from disease is the greatest gain. Good health, great wealth!" But they weren't referring merely to freedom from physical ailments such as toothaches. The spiritual disease that the Buddha referred to is the disease that causes the greatest suffering; it is the real disease. The cure of that disease must be correspondingly effective.

These days our usual escape from the disease is accidental. We escape without being aware of it, simply when the *dhammas* causing our suffering are replaced by *dhammas* that don't cause suffering. This is called "coincidental deliverance" (*tadaṅga-vimutti*). Coincidences come in various forms, including times when one disease replaces another. Nonetheless, don't ever forget that we escape from disease all the time in this ordinary, coincidental way, even while unaware of it.

On the occasions when we resolve to oversee the mind, it can be even more void and more free from spiritual disease than it is with accidental deliverance. At these times, because we keep the mind under control, there is deliverance by suppression (*vikkhambhana-vimutti*).

If we can deal with the disease absolutely and take out its root completely by removing the germ, this is called deliverance by cutting off (*samuccheda-vimutti*). This means we kill all the germs dead. It's not just a fluke or a temporary suppression.

Usually we experience at least the results of accidental deliverance (*tadaṅga-vimutti*), and that is already a big gain. If our peace of mind surpasses that, it is deliverance by suppression (*vikkham-bhana-vimutti*), or even deliverance by cutting off (*samuccheda-vimutti*), which is the highest level. If that point is reached, we no longer dwell in greed, hatred, delusion, and the various desires. Instead, we live with security, full of *sati-paññā* and free of suffering and agitation. Life is then like the freshness of innocent youth. There is full recovery from the spiritual disease.

We have completed all that needs to be studied, done, and experienced from our practice. Life is totally free of *dukkha*, both at the time of seeking and at the time of consuming. When we perform our daily tasks of seeking, including both our study and our jobs, there is no *dukkha*. When we receive the fruits, such as money, material wealth, status, prestige, and fame to enjoy, we have no *dukkha*. There is no *dukkha* in either kind of situation. We become truly exalted beings.

It's like catching a fish without getting caught by its sharp spines and then eating it without getting the bones stuck in the throat. Catching the fish there is no *dukkha*, and eating it there is no *dukkha*.

111

In conclusion, I would like to say again that this one subject of voidness covers all of Buddhism, for the Buddha breathed with *suññatā*. Voidness is the theory, the practice, and the fruit of the practice. If one studies, one must study *suññatā*; if one practices, it must be for the fruit of *suññatā*; and if one receives any fruit, it must be this *suññatā*, so that finally one attains the thing that is supremely desirable. There is nothing beyond voidness. When it is realized, all problems end.

Whether or not you understand, and whether or not you practice, must be your own responsibility. It is my duty only to explain the way things are. The knowing, the understanding, and the practice is the duty of each person.

If you think that the effort we have talked about is a good and true endeavor, then take it up. Renounce that which is cheap and poor in order to acquire that which is more valuable, most excellent. Keep up the work; don't let it fail. Make it develop and progress so as to benefit both yourself and all of humanity. Then you can feel sure that, in this life, you have done the best thing a human being can do, and have received the best thing a human being can receive. There is nothing beyond this. That's all there is.

Notes

PART I

1. Some key Pali terms, like "Dhamma," are not translated in the text. Others are only briefly translated. Please refer to the "Glossary of Pali Terms" for more complete translations of the Pali terms, which usually appear in parentheses in the text.

2. *Saṃyutta-nikāya, Mahāvāra-vagga, Sīsapāvana-sutta* (S. v. 438).

3. A contemporary of the Buddha and founder of the Jain religion.

4. The large body of material meant to explain the Theravāda Canon. These writings were begun a few centuries after the Buddha's passing, and then collected and recompiled around the fifth century CE.

5. Properly written *Pāli,* it is the language of the Theravāda Canon, believed to be the oldest record of the Buddha's life and teachings, along with the words and deeds of his disciples.

6. The famous *Ovādapātimokkha* (Chief of all Sayings): *Khuddaka-nikāya, Dhammapāda,* Verse 183, and D.ii.49.

7. *Majjhima-nikāya, Mūlapaṇṇāsa, Cūḷataṇhāsaṅkhaya-sutta* (M. i. 251). Also, *Saṃyutta-nikāya, Saḷāyatana-vagga, Dutiyaavijjāpahāna-sutta* (S. iv. 50).

8. Literally, "to bury oneself (one's mind) into."

9. The final words of the Buddha: *Digha-nikāya, Mahā-vagga, Parinibbāna-sutta* (D. ii. 156).

10. Ajahn Buddhadāsa translated *The Zen Teachings of Huang Po* (tr. John Blofeld, New York: Grove, 1959) into Thai.

11. This is the beginning line of the traditional Pali formula for taking refuge in the Buddha, Dhamma, and Sangha.

PART II

12. The Thai word for "study" or "education" is the Sanskrit-derived *sikṣa*, equivalent to the Pali *sikkhā* (training). For Ajahn Buddhadāsa, study or *sikṣa* carried the full sense of *sikkhā*: "look, look, look, until seeing; see, see, see, until knowing; know, know, know, until you can practice; then practice, practice, practice, until free of dukkha."

13. "One who is gone to *tathatā* (thusness, suchness)" or "One come from *tathatā*," the term used by the Buddha when referring to himself.

14. *Saṁyutta-nikāya, Mahāvāra-vagga, Sotāpatti-saṁyutta, Sappañña-vagga, Dhammadinna-sutta* (S. v. 407). Also, *Aṅguttara-nikāya, Duka-nipāta, Paṭhama-paṇṇāsaka, Parisa-vagga* (A.i.73), Sutta 6.

15. Ajahn Buddhadāsa felt that some Mahāyāna teachings on *suññatā* have gone beyond this practical understanding and become philosophical.

16. *Khuddaka-nikāya, Sutta-nipāta, Pārāyana-vagga, Mogharāja-sutta,* Verse 1119.

17. This is not a direct quote from the Buddha, as are other quotations here, but is a well-known saying in Thai Buddhism. It follows from, and is in line with, various statements made by the Buddha.

18. *Khuddaka-nikāya, Dhammapāda,* Verses 203–4.

19. *Majjhima-nikāya, Mūla-paṇṇāsa, Alagaddūpama-sutta* (M. i. 140).

20. We don't capitalize *dhamma* when we use it in this, its most ordinary, sense to mean "thing" or "nature."

21. *Saṁyutta-nikāya, Nidāna-vagga, Abhisamaya-saṁyutta, Mahā-*

vagga, Sutta 1 and 2 (S. ii. 92 and 95). The Pali Text Society translation has "approached" rather than "attach" or "cling."

22. *Khuddaka-nikāya, Udāna, Paṭhamanibbāna-sutta* (Ud 79).

23. *Majjhima-nikāya, Mūlapaṇṇāsa, Cūḷasīhanāda-sutta* (M. i. 66).

24. Ajahn Buddhadāsa used the Thai word *wun* as the opposite of *wāng* (void, empty, free). *Wun* means "busy," "fussy," "disordered," "worried," "disturbed," "tumultuous."

25. *Majjhima-nikāya, Uparipaṇṇāsa, Āṇañjasappāya-sutta* (M. ii. 263 f.).

26. *Dhammadinnā-sutta* (S. v. 407). See Note 14 above.

27. Entry into the stream that flows to *nibbāna*. This represents the attainment of the first stage of holiness through cutting the first three *saṃyojana* (fetters that bind beings to the cycles of becoming). The first three fetters are personality belief, doubt, and attachment to practices and rituals.

28. The wearing of charms to ward off dangers is a superstitious practice common in Thailand. The charms are often associated with "powerful" or "holy" Buddha images.

29. *Lakkhaṇa* can be translated as "feature," "mark," "sign," "characteristic" or "character," "quality," "attribute," "property," "essence."

30. See *nirodha* in the glossary.

31. *Majjhima-nikaya, Uparipaṇṇāsa, Uppaṇṇasaka-sutta* (M. iii. 294).

32. *Majjhima-nikāya, Uparipaṇṇāsa, Cūḷasuññatā-sutta* (M. iii. 104).

33. Devoid of *nimitta* (signs, marks, mentally created distinctions).

34. *Majjhima-nikāya, Upari-paṇṇāsa, Cūḷasuññatā-sutta* (M. iii. 104 ff.).

35. *Majjhima-nikāya, Mūla-paṇṇāsa, Satipaṭṭhāna-sutta* (M. i. 59).

36. These are the four foundations of mindfulness, all of which can be "developed and made much of" through the practice of *ānāpānasati*. See *Majjhima-nikāya, Ānāpānasati-sutta* (M. ii. 83 ff.).

37. *Aṅguttara-nikāya, Tika-nipāta, Tatiyapaṇṇāsaka, Sambodhi-vagga, Nidāna-sutta* (A.i.263).

38. Aṅgulimāla was a notorious bandit and murderer. His name came from the necklace (*māla*) he wore, which was made of fingers (*aṅgula*) cut from his victims. Needless to say, the Buddha

wasn't terrified like everyone else. See *Majjhima-nikāya, Majjhima-paṇṇāsa, Aṅgulimāla-sutta* (M. ii. 99).

39. The Indian religious tradition whose teachings are considered to be the essence of the Vedas, the ancient scriptures of the Hindus.

40. *Saṁyutta-nikāya, Mahāvāra-vagga, Samādhi-sutta* (S. v. 414).

41. The Sixth Ch'an Patriarch in China. Ajahn Buddhadāsa's translation of his "Platform Sutra" was the first Zen work to appear in the Thai language.

PART III

42. *Paṭicca-samuppāda* can be understood on two levels. First, it is the universal law of nature. All things arise, exist, and cease through dependent co-origination. More specifically, and this is the sense in which the Buddha usually used the term, it is the dependent origination of *dukkha*, together with the dependent quenching of *dukkha*. *Dukkha* is quenched when all of its conditions are quenched, particularly the originating condition of ignorance (*avijjā*). The Buddha's awakening centered on this realization (Vin. i. 1 f.).

The distinction between these two levels is crucial, because all life is a process of dependent co-origination. We might ask, does stopping dependent co-origination mean stopping life? No. We simply seek to stop the conditioning by ignorance that leads to *dukkha*. The natural flow of conditioning of the psycho-physical universe is not a problem to be stopped. Rather, we let it flow naturally when we stop attaching to it through ignorant contact and its consequences. To simplify the distinction, we use the term *idappacca-yatā* (conditionality) for the natural conditioning of the material world and restrict *paṭicca-samuppāda* to the conditioning of *dukkha* within the human mind, which is under the power of *avijjā*.

Paṭicca-samuppāda, as it is discussed here, always implies ignorance. The original condition for the process is *avijjā*, which then makes contact ignorant, makes feeling ignorant, and so on. In fact, craving, clinging, becoming, and birth can only be ignorant.

Although *dukkha* is the spur of wisdom, it itself is ignorant, too. *Dukkha* can arise only in the ignorant mind.

Many authorities insist that if there is *phassa*, *vedanā* must automatically follow. They would not agree with Ajahn Buddhadāsa's statement that dependent origination can be stopped at contact and that feeling can be prevented. Although he admitted that it is extremely difficult, Ajahn Buddhadāsa insisted that a highly trained mind can keep contact as mere contact through *sati-paññā*, without it giving rise to feeling of any sort (including the so-called "neutral feeling"). Those who doubt this possibility should carefully consider the Buddha's advice to Bāhiya quoted later in this chapter.

Nonetheless, should *vedanā* arise, all is not lost. Mindfulness and wisdom, if they recover quickly, can stop the stream of dependent origination at feeling and prevent craving. That's the last chance. Should craving arise, *dukkha* is certain and the best one can do is to drop that *dukkha* as quickly as possible, which still requires enough *sati-paññā* to supplant the ignorance that has stirred up the whole mess.

43. *Khuddaka-nikāya, Udāna, Bodhi-vagga, Bāhiya-sutta* (Ud 6).
44. *Digha-nikāya, Mahā-vagga, Parinibbāna-sutta* (D. ii. 151).
45. *Saṁyutta-nikāya, Mahāvāra-vagga, Indrīya-saṁyutta, Sūkara-khātā-vagga, Sūkarakhātā-sutta* (S. v. 234). Note that this is a Pali word, not to be confused with the Sanskrit *yoga*, which means "spiritual endeavor."
46. *Visuddhimagga*, xvi, 90.
47. It is common to find the word *sampajañña* used to mean "worldly wisdom," e.g., knowing how to function within a certain cultural context or knowing how to fix a flat tire. We should never forget that the wisdom the Buddha teaches is the one that quenches *dukkha*. We prefer to understand *sampajañña* as seeing the impermanence, unsatisfactoriness, selflessness, voidness, etc., of a specific experience, including all its physical and mental components.

48. "A shining one," a celestial being, from roots meaning "to shine" and "of the sky."
49. The full and new moon days when laypeople would gather at temples and religious places to keep the eight precepts of virtuous conduct.

Glossary of Pali Terms

Abhidhamma. Higher Dhamma, extra Dhamma: the third of three "baskets" of the Buddhist Canon. Compiled after the Buddha's death, they are a complex analysis of mind and matter into their constituent parts. Though it is often translated as "higher Dhamma," Ajahn Buddhadāsa calls it "excess Dhamma." He says that the real *Abhidhamma* is found in the *Sutta-piṭaka* (the Buddha's discourses): teachings such as *paṭicca-samuppāda*, *tathatā*, and *suññatā*.

Ahaṁkāra. "I-ing," "I-making," egoism: having or making the feeling of "I." A stronger, cruder sense of ego. [See 'I' and 'Mine' in Chapter 2.]

Ānāpānasati. Mindfulness with breathing in and out: the only meditation or *vipassanā* system expressly taught by the Buddha, it covers all four foundations of mindfulness and perfects the seven factors of awakening, leading to liberation. Ajahn Buddhadāsa considers it the best way to realize *suññatā*.

Aniccaṁ. Impermanent (or *aniccatā*, impermanence), flux, instability: conditioned things are ever-changing, constantly arising, manifesting, and ceasing. This is the first fundamental characteristic (*lakkhaṇa*) of conditioned things.

119

Anattā. Not-self (or *anattatā*, selflessness, soullessness): the fact that all things, without exception and including *nibbāna*, are not-self and lack any essence or substance that could properly be regarded as a "self." This fact does not deny the existence of things, but denies that they can be owned or controlled, that they can be the owner or controller, in any but a relative, conventional sense. This is the third fundamental characteristic of conditioned things.

Anupādisesa-nibbāna-dhātu. The *nibbāna* element (*dhātu*) with no fuel remaining: the *nibbāna* element experienced by the Arahant in whom all defilement is ended and the feelings are cooled, that is, are not regarded as positive or negative.

Anupassanā. Contemplation, spiritual experience: following up (and penetrating more deeply into) insight. Sustained, nonverbal, non-reactive, evenminded scrutiny of a *dhamma*. Three specific contemplations are listed below and four more are described in the glossary entry for *satipaṭṭhāna*. [See "In Touch with *Suññatā*" in Chapter 9.]

> *anattānupassana.* The contemplation of not-self, spiritual experiences of not-self: seeing that there is no self nor anything belonging to self, that there are merely *dhammas* and natural processes.

> *dukkhānupassanā.* Contemplation of the characteristic of dukkha in objects of attachment.

> *suññatānupassanā.* Spiritual experience of *suññatā*.

Arahant. Worthy One, one far from defilement, one who has broken the wheel of birth and death, one without secrets: the mind totally and finally free of greed, anger, and delusion; void of "I" and "mine"; which has ended *kamma*; which is unaffected by dukkha. The Arahant should not be regarded as a "person" or "individual." "Arahantship" is an English contrivance meaning "the state of being Arahant."

Ariyasacca. Noble truth: truth that frees one from enemies (*ari*), namely, defilements and *dukkha*. Usually expressed in the fourfold formula: the noble truth of *dukkha*, that is, the fact that *dukkha* exists; the noble truth of *dukkha-samudaya* (the origin of *dukkha*), namely, *taṇhā* (or the conditions of *paṭicca-samuppāda*); the noble truth of *dukkha-nirodha* (the quenching of *dukkha*), by quenching *taṇhā*, including ignorance and all the conditions of *paṭicca-samuppāda*; and the noble truth of *dukkha-nirodhagāminī paṭipadā* (the practice leading to the quenching of *dukkha*). Although the traditional formula is fourfold, Truth is but One, there is no second.

Asaṅkhata. The unconditioned, the unconcocted: that which is unborn, uncreated, undying, unchanging, beyond causes and conditions, and timeless, i.e., *nibbāna*. [See *saṅkhata*.]

Āsava. Discharges, outflows, leaks, eruptions: the mental defilements that flow out from the mind's depths in response to conditions. After the tendencies toward defilement (*anusaya*) build up, their pressure leaks out more or less strongly depending on conditions. The three *āsavas* are listed as the eruptions of sense desire, of becoming (or existence), and of ignorance. Sometimes the eruption of views is added in the third position. Awakening is often expressed as the end of the *āsava*.

Attā. Self, ego, soul (Sanskrit, *atman*): the instinctual feeling (and illusion) that there is some "I" who does all the things to be done in life. Through ignorance and wrong understanding this instinctual sensibility is attached to and becomes "ego." Although theories about "self" abound, all are mere speculations about something that exists only in our imaginations. In a conventional sense, the *attā* can be a useful concept (belief, perception), but that conventional "self" is not-self (*anattā*). No personal, independent, self-existing, free-willing, lasting substance or essence can be found anywhere, whether within or without human life and experience, not even in "God." [Compare *anattā*, *idappaccayatā*, and *suññatā*.]

Avijjā. Ignorance, not-knowing, wrong knowledge, foolishness: the lack, partial or total, of *vijjā* (correct knowledge) regarding the things that need to be known (e.g., the Four Noble Truths, *paṭicca-samuppāda, suññatā*); also knowing things in the wrong way, that is, as permanent, satisfying, and self. The most original cause of all *dukkha*. Without Dhamma practice, ignorance grows into increasingly wrong knowledge.

Āyatana. Senses, sense media, experienceables: things that are experienced or sensed, most commonly, the inner *āyatana* (eyes, ears, nose, tongue, body, and mind-sense) and outer *āyatana* (forms, sounds, odors, flavors, touches, and mental objects). Also, applied to the formless meditations (e.g., *viññāṇañcāyatana*) in that they are objects of experience. Lastly, *nibbāna* is called an *āyatana* in that it can be experienced. [See "Burning *Dhammas*" in Chapter 5 as well as "Steps of *Suññatā*" and "Liberated into Voidness" in Chapter 9.]

Bhava. Becoming, being, existence: gestation of the ego-to-be in the womb of ignorance. There are three realms of becoming: sensual (*kāma-bhava*), fine-material (*rūpa-bhava*), and immaterial (*arū-pa-bhava*). To understand *bhava* in literal, physical terms is to miss the spiritual point. *Nibbāna* is beyond all levels of *bhava*. [See the first three sections in Chapter 10.]

Buddha-sāsanā. The teachings of Buddhas, Buddhism: now used in the modern sense of "religion." The terms commonly used by the Buddha were *Dhamma-Vinaya* (doctrine and discipline), *brahmacariya* (sublime or highest living), and *saddhamma* (the Good Dhamma). [See the first few paragraphs of Chapter 1.]

Citta. Mind, heart, consciousness, mind-heart: that which thinks, knows, and experiences, the four mental *khandhas*. In a more limited sense, *citta* is what "thinks," can be defiled by *kilesa*, can be developed, and can realize *nibbāna*. Although we cannot know *citta* directly, it is where all Dhamma practice occurs.

Its fundamental nature is voidness. [See "All Practices in One" in Chapter 4.]

Dāna. Giving, generosity, charity: a fundamental virtue and practice. [See "All Practices in One" in Chapter 4.]

Deva. Shining one, celestial being, heavenly: a being enjoying the life of leisure in which sensual pleasures come without having to work and sweat for them as humans (*manussa*) must do.

Dhamma. Truth, Nature, Law, Natural Truth, Duty, Order, "the way things are": this impossible-to-translate word has many meanings, the most important of which are Nature, the Law of Nature, our Duty according to Natural Law, and the Fruits of doing that Duty correctly according to Natural Law. [See *dhamma* and *paṭicca-samuppāda*.]

dhamma. Thing, nature, natural thing: all things, mental and physical, conditioned and unconditioned, are *dhammas*. There are *nāma-dhammas* (immaterial things, mental things) and *rūpadhammas* (material things, tangible things). [See *Dhamma*, the first paragraphs in Chapter 5, and "Really Knowing" in Chapter 8.]

Dhātu. Element, natural essence: something that maintains itself temporarily or permanently, through conditions or independent of them, depending on the kind of *dhātu* it is. Often, but not exclusively, *dhātu* refers to an inherent potential within nature that is not at the moment Dhammically active, which manifests or functions, or not, depending on conditions. Some important kinds of elements are listed below. [See Chapter 7 and "In Touch with *Suññatā*" in Chapter 9.]

ākāsa-dhātu. Space element.

amata-dhātu. Deathless element.

arūpa-dhātu. Formless element, element of immateriality.

nekkhama-dhātu. Renunciation element.

nibbāna-dhātu. Coolness element.

nirodha-dhātu. Quenching element.

rūpa-dhātu. Form element, element of materiality.

suññatā-dhātu. Voidness element.

vatthu-dhātu. Material element.

viññāṇa-dhātu. Consciousness element.

Dosa. Hatred, ill-will: the second category of defilement (*kilesa*), which includes anger, aversion, dislike, and all other negative thoughts and emotions. It is characterized by the mind pushing away the object. *Kodha* (anger) is often used interchangeably with *dosa*.

Dukkha. Pain, hurt, ill-being, suffering, misery (or *dukkhatā*, unsatisfactoriness, imperfection): the spiritual dilemma of human beings. Etymologically, *dukkha* can be translated "hard to endure, difficult to bear"; "once seen, it is ugly"; and "horribly, wickedly void." In its experiential sense, *dukkha* is the quality of experience that results when the mind is concocted by *avijjā* into desire, attachment, egoism, and selfishness. This feeling takes on forms—from the crudest to the most subtle levels—such as disappointment, dissatisfaction, frustration, agitation, anguish, disease, despair. In its universal sense, *dukkhatā* is the inherent condition of unsatisfactoriness, imperfection, and misery in all impermanent, conditioned things (*saṅkhāra*). This second fundamental characteristic of conditioned things is a result of *aniccatā* (the fact of impermanence); impermanent things cannot satisfy our wants and desires no matter how hard we try (or cry), and trying is often very hard. Further, the

124

inherent undependability, decay, and dissolution of things is painfully ugly. To fully understand the meaning of *dukkha*, one must realize that *sukha* (happiness, bliss) is also *dukkha*. *Nibbāna* (i.e., *suññatā*) is the only thing that is not *dukkha*. [See "Greed, Hatred, and Delusion" in Chapter 2.]

Hiri. Shame, embarrassment: to be ashamed of doing evil, which prevents one from doing it. *Hiri* is nothing like guilt. The supreme level of *hiri* is disgust with *dukkha*.

Idappaccayatā. Conditionality, the "fact of having this as condition." The universal law of nature applying to all phenomena. All things happen, change, and pass away according to causes and conditions. This natural reality is a central thread running through all the Buddha's Dhamma, such as in the four ennobling truths. *Paṭiccasamuppāda* is the specific case of the conditioned arising of dukkha and its quenching. (Please see entry.)

Iddhipāda. Roads to success; paths to, or bases of, accomplishment: *chanda*, will, aspiration, resolve in carrying out an activity or duty; *viriya*, energy, effort, exertion in that duty without letting up; *citta*, attentiveness, thoughtfulness regarding that duty; *vimaṁsā*, investigation and examination of, reasoning about that duty.

Jarāmaraṇa. Decay and death, aging and death. Ajahn Buddhadāsa points to the ego-structure's inevitable decay and death every time ego-formation occurs, which is the suffering addressed by the Buddha's path (more so than physical aging and death).

Jāti. Birth: this term has a literal meaning and a Dhamma or spiritual meaning. The first is physical birth of an infant from its mother's womb. The second meaning, the Dhammically significant one, is mental birth of the ego, the "I Am," through the process of dependent origination. There is no linguistic or Dhammic justification for translating *jāti* as "rebirth." [See "The Meaning of Birth" in Chapter 8 and "Spiritual Birth" in Chapter 10.]

Jhāna. Peering, contemplation, absorption, meditation: unification of the mind focused on an object to develop tranquility or on impermanence for the sake of insight. *Jhāna* is understood both as an activity of the mind (focusing, peering) and as the result of that activity. These results are of two types: (1) the *rūpajhānas*, the *jhānas* dependent on the forms of material objects, mental absorption into objects of finer materiality, and (2) the *arūpas*, the *jhānas* dependent on immaterial or formless objects. The *jhānas* are listed below. The first four are the *rūpajhānas*, and the second four are the *arūpas*.

paṭhama-jhāna, which has five factors: noting (the object), experiencing (the object), rapture, joy, and one-pointedness.

dutiya-jhāna, which has three factors: rapture, joy, and one-pointedness.

tatiya-jhāna, which has two factors: joy and one-pointedness.

catuttha-jhāna, which has two factors: equanimity and one-pointedness.

ākāsānañcāyatana, which is the experience of infinite space.

viññāṇañcāyatana, which is the experience of infinite consciousness.

ākiñcaññāyatana, which is the experience of infinite nothingness.

nevasaññānāsaññāyatana, which is the experience that is neither-experience-nor-nonexperience.

Kamma. Action (Sanskrit, *karma*): actions of body, speech, and mind due to wholesome and unwholesome volitions. Good intentions and actions bring good results, bad intentions and actions bring bad results. Unintentional actions are not *kamma*, are not Dhammically significant. *Kamma* has nothing to do with fate, luck, or fortune, nor does it mean the result of *kamma*. The Buddha taught the end of *kamma*. "The *kamma* that ends all *kamma*" is

126

the Noble Eightfold Path that ends the "doer" (*attā*). [See *kamma-vipāka*.]

Kamma-bhava. Action of becoming, active process of becoming: the action that brings into existence, the result of which is *uppatti-bhava*, the state of existence that arises.

Kamma-vipāka. Result of action, *kamma*-fruit: the happiness (heaven) and sadness (hell) arising from "good" and "bad" intentions. [See "Spiritual Birth" in Chapter 10.]

Kataññū-katavedī. Gratitude and grateful action: knowing that something has benefitted one and feeling correspondingly grateful, then responding properly in thought, speech, and deed.

Khandha. Aggregates, heaps, groups: the five subsystems or basic functions that constitute the human being. These groups are not entities in themselves, they are merely categories into which all aspects of our lives can be analyzed. None of them are "self," "of self," "in self," or "my self"; they have nothing to do with "selfhood" and there is no "self" apart from them. When they attach or are attached to, the five are known as the *upādāna-khandha* (aggregates of attachment). *Nibbāna* is the only thing not covered by the five *khandha*. The five are:

rūpa-khandha. Form-aggregate, particularly the body, its nervous system, and sense objects (the world).

vedanā-khandha. Feeling-aggregate. [Compare *vedanā*.]

saññā-khandha. Recognition-aggregate; the discrimination, labelling, and evaluation of sense experience. [Compare *saññā*.]

saṅkhāra-khandha. Thought-aggregate; thought processes and emotions, including volition, desire, attachment, and "birth."

viññāṇa-khandha. Consciousness-aggregate; the bare knowing of a sense object, the most primitive function of mind through which physical sense stimulation becomes conscious (although often without awareness).

Khanti. Patience, endurance, forbearance, tolerance: to accept and endure defilements (rather than repress them) regarding people, circumstances, and the difficulties of Dhamma practice until they are understood and released. The Buddha called *khanti* "the supreme way to burn up defilements."

Khema. Security: freedom from bondage, from the yokes (*yoga*).

Kilesa. Defilements, impurities: all the things that dull, darken, dirty, defile, and sadden the *citta*. The three primary categories of *kilesa* are *lobha* (or *rāga*), *dosa*, and *moha*. [See "Greed, Hatred, and Delusion" in Chapter 2 and separate glossary entries for *lobha*, *dosa*, and *moha*.]

Lobha. Greed: the first category of defilement (*kilesa*), which includes erotic love, lust, miserliness, and all other positive thoughts and emotions. A common synonym is *rāga* (lust).

Magga-phala. Path and fruition: there are four paths leading to "nobility," i.e., the insight knowledges that cut through the fetters (*saṁyojana*), and there are four corresponding fruitions arising from those paths (*magga*) cutting through defilement. The four paths and fruitions are the attainment and experience, respectively, of the stages of Stream-Enterer, Once-Returner, Non-Returner, and Arahant. Each has its own level of *nibbāna* or "coolness."

Mahāpurisavihāra. The abode of the Great Person. [See the first paragraphs in Chapter 9.]

Mamaṁkāra. "My-ing," "mine-making," selfishness: having or making the feeling of "my" and "mine." A stronger, cruder sense of attachment and possession arising from "I-ing." [See 'I' and 'Mine' in Chapter 2.]

Māyā. Illusion: not necessarily meaning something that doesn't exist at all, but something that is seen incorrectly, without insight into its true nature. For example, "self" exists as a concept but not as a reality in itself; therefore, it is illusory, imagined, or delusive.

Moha. Delusion: the third category of defilement (*kilesa*), which includes fear, worry, confusion, doubt, infatuation, expectation, longing after the past, and guilt. It is characterized by the mind spinning around the object.

Muni. Sage.

Nibbāna. Coolness, quenching: the Absolute, the Supreme, the Ultimate Reality in Buddhism; the "goal" of Buddhist practice, and the highest potential of humanity. *Nibbāna* manifests when the fires of defilement, attachment, selfishness, and *dukkha* are cooled. When they are permanently cooled, *nibbāna* manifests perfectly, totally, timelessly. Not a place, for *nibbāna* is beyond existence and non-existence, not even a state of mind, for *nibbāna* is neither mental nor physical, but a *dhamma* the mind can realize and experience. *Nibbāna* is to be realized in this life. In Pali, the root of *nibbāna* has verb forms meaning "to cool, to quench, to extinguish." [*Nibbana* is discussed throughout this book. The following are a few of the sections in which it is discussed: "The Meaning of *Suññatā*" in Chapter 4, "All Nature Is *Suññatā*" in Chapter 5, "Unsurpassable *Suññatā*" and "In Touch with *Suññatā*" in Chapter 9, "Being Happy" in Chapter 12, and "The Last Chance" in Chapter 13.]

Nimitta. Sign, image, mark, characteristic. In meditation, a mentally created image arising due to concentration. Also, the signs or characteristics of objects that are the mentally created distinctions to which the mind clings.

Nirodha. Quenching, cessation, extinction: occurring when something is thoroughly calmed, cooled, and quenched such that it won't concoct, heat up, or become the basis for *dukkha* again. The ordinary, temporary cessation of something is called *atthaṅgama*. To emphasize the finality of *nirodha*, Ajahn Buddhadāsa refers to it as "remainderless quenching."

Ottappa. Moral fear, moral dread: wisely to fear the consequences of doing evil. Moral dread keeps one from doing wrong, unlike guilt, which is after the fact. The supreme level of *ottappa* is fear of *dukkha*.

Paññā. Wisdom, insight, intuitive understanding: correct seeing, knowing, understanding, experiencing of the things we must know in order to quench *dukkha*, namely, the Four Noble Truths, the three characteristics, dependent origination, and voidness. The various terms used for "knowing" are not meant to express an intellectual activity, although the intellect has its role. The emphasis is on direct, intuitive, nonconceptual comprehending of life as it is here and now. Memory, language, and thought are not required. *Paññā*, rather than faith or will power, is the characteristic quality of Buddhism.

Pāpa. Evil, vice, demerit.

Paṭicca-samuppāda. Dependent co-origination, interdependent co-origination, conditioned co-arising: the profound and detailed causal process or flow that concocts *dukkha*; also the description of this process. Following is the main sequence. The *ākāra* (modes or conditions) listed below are explained separately in this glossary.

Dependent on sense organ and sense object, arises consciousness (*viññāṇa*).

The meeting of these three is contact (*phassa*).

Dependent on contact, feeling (*vedanā*) occurs.

Dependent on feeling, desire (*taṇhā*) occurs.

Dependent on desire, attachment (*upādana*) occurs.

Dependent on attachment, becoming (*bhava*) occurs.

Dependent on becoming, birth (*jāti*) occurs.

Dependent on birth, decay and death (*jāramaraṇa*) occur.

Sorrow, lamentation, pain, grief, and despair thus exist fully. The arising of the whole mess of *dukkha* happens in just this way. [See "Dependent Co-arising" in Chapter 10.]

Phassa. The meeting and working together of sense organ, sense object, and sense consciousness (*viññāṇa*). When a sensual stimulus makes enough of an impact upon the mind to draw a response, either ignorant or wise, beginning with *vedanā*.

Puñña. Goodness, virtue, merit.

Rāga. Lust: desire to get or have. *Rāga* can be sexual, for material objects, and even for nonmaterial things. Poetically, covers all attachment and defilement. [See *lobha.*]

Rishi. Seer.

Sacca. Honesty, truthfulness, truth.

Samādhi. Concentration, collectedness: secure establishment of the mind, the gathering together of the mental flow. Proper *samādhi* has the qualities of purity, clarity, stability, calmness, readiness, and gentleness. It is perfected in one-pointedness (*ekagattā*) and *jhāna*. The supreme *samādhi* is the one-pointed mind (*ekagattā-citta*), which has *nibbāna* as its sole concern. In a broader sense, *samādhi* can be translated "meditation," meaning development of the mind through the power of *samādhi*.

Samuccheda-pahāna. Abandonment through cutting off, final abandonment: the final and total elimination of the defilements by cutting them off at their roots.

Saṁyojana. Fetters, bonds: the ten defilements that keep us trapped in the cycles of egoistic birth and death. The ten are personality belief, doubt, attachment to practices and rituals, sensual desire, ill-will, lust for material things, lust for nonmaterial things, conceit, agitation, and ignorance. The "Stream Enterer" severs the first three and the Arahant destroys them all.

Saṅkhata. The conditioned, concocted, produced, created: applied to all things that are impermanent, that arise and pass away, and that are subject to the law of *idappaccayatā.* [See *asaṅkhata.*]

Saññā. Recognition, perception, experience, evaluation: once the mind has made contact (*phassa*) with a sense object and then feels it (*vedanā*), a concept, label, or image is attached to the experience, which involves recognizing similarities with past experience and discriminating the value of the object. Sometimes, the word *saññā* is used in a general way roughly equivalent to "experience," as in *āraññasaññā,* recognition of "just forest" and *pathavīsaññā,* recognition of "just earth." [See "Steps of *Suññatā*" in Chapter 9.]

Sati. Mindfulness, attention, awareness, recall, recollection: the mind's ability to know and observe itself. *Sati* is the vehicle and transport mechanism for *paññā.* Without *sati,* wisdom cannot be developed, retrieved, or applied. *Sati* is not memory or remembering, although it is related to them. Nor is it mere heedfulness or carefulness. *Sati* allows us to be aware of what we are about to do. It is characterized by speed and agility. In Thai, *sati* is translated as *raluek,* which can be rendered as "recall" or, perhaps, "recollection." This is a sense of *sati* that is often overlooked. The awareness recalls or brings back wisdom. This recall is not the same as memory, for it does not recall concepts or beliefs, but is rather intuitive wisdom that is experienced instead of thought.

Sati-paññā. Mindfulness and wisdom: *sati* and *paññā* must work together. *Paññā* depends on *sati.* Wisdom arises through mindfulness of life's experiences and is applied to present experience through mindfulness. Yet, without sufficient wisdom, mindfulness would be misused. In everyday Thai, *sati-paññā* has come to mean "intelligence." When Ajahn Buddhadāsa uses it in this sense, it is translated accordingly.

Satipaṭṭhāna. The four foundations or applications of mindfulness: the four bases on which *sati* must be established in mental development. We investigate life through these four subjects of spiritual study:

kāyānupassanā. Contemplation of body (in bodies).

vedanānupassanā. Contemplation of feeling (in feelings).

cittānupassanā. Contemplation of mind (in mind states).

dhammānupassanā. Contemplation of Dhamma (in *dhammas*).

Sati-sampajañña. Mindfulness and self-awareness: similar to *sati-paññā*, the difference lying in the meaning of *sampajañña*, which is ready comprehension, clear comprehension, or wisdom-in-action. Whereas *paññā* is developed, or "stored up," through introspection and insight, *sampajañña* is the immediate and specific application of wisdom to, and into, a particular situation or experience. Whereas *paññā* understands that "everything is void," *sampajañña* understands that "this is void." All understanding relies on mindfulness for its appearance, recall, and application.

Sa-upādisesa-nibbāna-dhātu. The *nibbāna* element with fuel remaining: the *nibbāna* element experienced by the Arahant in whom all defilement is ended but whose feelings are not yet cooled, that is, whose feelings are still regarded as being positive and negative.

Sīla. Normality, morality, right conduct: verbal and bodily action in line with Dhamma, the way of living in society that is truly peaceful because it does no harm. Much more than following rules or precepts, true *sīla* comes from wisdom and is undertaken joyfully. [See "All Practices in One" in Chapter 4.]

Sīlabbataparāmāsa. Superstition, attachment to practices and rituals: to ignorantly fondle practices, precepts, rites, and rituals; to do anything for the wrong reason. Even a correct practice can be misused in this way.

Soracca. Gentleness, meekness, modesty.

Suññatā. Voidness: all things, without any exception, are void of "self" and "belonging to self," are void of any meaning or value of "self," are void and free of "I" and "mine." *Suññatā* is an inherent quality or characteristic of everything, including "Ultimate Reality," "God," and *nibbāna.* *Suññatā* also refers to the mind that is free of attachment, which is void of greed, anger, and delusion. *Nibbāna* is the "supreme voidness," free and void of *attā* and *attanīyā,* void of ignorance, desire, attachment, ego, defilement, and *dukkha.* [See "The Meaning of *Suññatā*" in Chapter 4 and the Editor's Note on the translation of *Suññatā.*]

Sutta. Discourse: literally, "thread." The term is used, in Theravāda Buddhism, for discourses attributed to the Buddha and certain of his disciples.

Taṇhā. Desire, craving, thirst, blind want: *taṇhā* is always ignorant and should not be confused with "wise want" (*sammā-sankappa,* right aspiration). The Buddha distinguished three kinds of desire: sensual desire; desire for being (having, becoming); and desire for not being (not having). Conditioned by foolish *vedanā,* *taṇhā* in turn concocts *upādāna.*

Tathāgata. One gone to Thusness, Thus-gone-one, Thus-come-one: the term used by the Buddha when referring to himself. Also used, occasionally, when referring to Arahants in general.

Tathatā. Thusness, suchness, just-like-that-ness: neither this nor that, the reality of nonduality. Things are just as they are (void) regardless of our perceptions, likes and dislikes, suppositions and beliefs, hopes and memories.

Tilakkhaṇa. Three characteristics, three marks of existence: inherent features of all conditioned things, namely, the facts of impermanence (*aniccatā*), unsatisfactoriness (*dukkhatā*), and not-self (*anattatā*).

Tipiṭaka. The "three baskets" of scriptures: the *Vinaya* (discipline for monks and nuns), the *Sutta* (discourse of the Buddha and leading disciples), and the *Abhidhamma* (psycho-philosophical texts). Called "baskets" after the containers that held the original palm leaf manuscripts.

Tiratana. Triple Gem: the Buddha, Dhamma, and Sangha. [See *tisaraṇa.*]

Tisaraṇa. Three refuges: the Buddha, Dhamma, and Sangha. On the ordinary level the refuges are external: Buddha (the man who lived 2,500 years ago), his teaching, and his realized disciples. More immediate refuges are found internally: the inherent ability to know truth and be awake, the reality of *paṭicca-samuppāda*, and right practice according to the Dhamma known by Buddha. Also known as *Tiratana* (Triple Gem).

Upādana. Attachment, clinging, grasping: to hold on to something foolishly, to regard things as "I" and "mine," to take things personally. Not the things attached to, but the lustful-satisfaction (*chanda-rāga*) regarding them. The Buddha distinguished four kinds of *upādana*: attachment to sensuality, to views, to precepts and practices, and to words concerning self. Note that to hold something wisely is *samādāna*. [See the first three sections in Chapter 10.]

Vaṭṭasaṁsāra. Cycles of wandering, cycles of birth and death: the wandering, due to ignorance and attachment, through ego births (see *jāti*) and deaths.

Vedanā. Feeling: the mental reaction to or coloring of sense experience (*phassa*). Feeling comes in three forms: pleasant or agreeable (*sukhavedanā*), unpleasant or painful (*dukkha-vedanā*), and indeterminate, neither-unpleasant-nor-pleasant (*adukkhama-sukhavedanā*). *Vedanā* is a mental factor and should not be confused with physical sensations. This primitive activity of mind is not emotion, which is far more complex and involves thought, or the more complicated aspects of "feeling," as this word is understood in English. [See Chapter 10.]

Vihāra. Dwelling, abode, home.

Vijjā. Right knowledge, insight, wisdom: to know things as they really are, that is, to know them as impermanent, unsatisfactory, and not-self—void. *Vijjā* uproots, destroys, and replaces *avijjā*. [See "Ignorance of *Suññatā*" in Chapter 5.]

Vimutti. Deliverance, emancipation, salvation: if there is no qualifying adjective, *vimutti* means total, final release from egoistic existence and *dukkha*. However, we can distinguish the three levels of deliverance listed below. [See "Liberated into Voidness" in Chapter 9.]

tadaṅga-vimutti. Coincidental, accidental, or spontaneous deliverance. This happens naturally without any practical effort on our part, when we are distracted from or forget our current problem or attachment. While it helps us to stay relatively sane, it is not enough to bring lasting peace and happiness.

vikkhambana-vimutti. Deliverance by suppression. Through practical effort we keep the mind from developing defiled states. This brings greater but not total peace, freedom, and coolness.

samuccheda-vimutti. Deliverance by cutting off. We sever and uproot the defilements through the power of the transcendent path, so that no more defilement is ever possible again. This brings lasting and timeless peace, freedom, and coolness: what is commonly called "enlightenment."

Viññāṇa. Consciousness: knowing sense objects through the six doors (eyes, ears, etc.). The most basic mental activity required

136

for participation in the sensual world (*loka*), without it there is no experience.

Vipassanā. Insight, seeing clearly: to see directly into the true nature of things, i.e., *aniccatā, dukkhatā*, and *anattatā*, also, *paṭicca-samuppāda, tathatā*, and, of course, *suññatā*. *Vipassanā* popularly means mental development practiced for the sake of insight. In such cases, the theory and technique of particular practices must not be confused with actual experience of impermanence.

Yathābhūta-ñāṇadassana. Knowing and seeing things as they really are: synonymous with insight (*vipassanā*).

Yoga. Yoke, bond (Sanskrit, *yoga, yuga*). Often in Pali, *yoga* is used as a synonym for *āsava* [see above]. Sometimes, however, it has the more familiar meaning "spiritual endeavor, application, undertaking, effort," from the root meaning of "yoking, or being yoked," that is, "connected."

Yogi. Adept, one full of effort, devotee: one "yoked" through effort to some mental object or spiritual goal.

Buddhadāsa Will Never Die

Buddhadāsa will never die.
Even when the body dies, it will not listen,
whether it is or is not is of no consequence,
it is only something passing through time.

Buddhadāsa carries on, there's no dying.
However good or bad the times,
one with the true teaching.
Having offered body and mind in ceaseless service
Under Lord Buddha's command.

Buddhadāsa lives on, there's no dying.
In service to all humanity forever
through the Dhamma proclamations left behind—
O Friends, can't you see!
What dies?

Even when I die and the body ceases
my voice still echoes in comrades' ears
clear and bright, as loud as ever.

Just as if I never died
the Dhamma-body lives on.

Treat me as if I never died,
as though I am with you all as before.
Speak up whatever is on your minds
as if I sit with you helping point out the facts.

Treat me as if I never died,
then many streams of benefits will accrue.
Don't forget the days set aside for Dhamma discussion,
Realize the absolute and stop dying!

Buddhadāsa Bhikkhu
1987

About the Author

BUDDHADĀSA BHIKKHU (Slave of the Buddha) went forth as a *bhikkhu* (Buddhist monk) in 1926, at the age of twenty. After a few years of study in Bangkok, he was inspired to live close to nature in order to investigate the Buddha-Dhamma as the Buddha had done. Thus, he established Suan Mokkhabalārāma (The Garden of the Power of Liberation) in 1932, near his home town in southern Thailand. At that time, it was the only forest Dhamma center in the region, and one of a very few places dedicated to *vipassanā* (meditation leading to "seeing clearly" into reality). Word of Buddhadāsa Bhikkhu and Suan Mokkh has spread over the years, so that his life and work are considered to be among the most influential events in the Buddhist history of Siam. Here, we can only mention a few of the more memorable services he has rendered to Buddhism.

Ajahn Buddhadāsa worked painstakingly to establish and explain the correct and essential principles of pristine Buddhism. That work was based on extensive research of the Pali texts (Canon and commentary), especially of the Buddha's discourses (*sutta piṭaka*), followed by personal experiment and practice with these teachings. From this, he uncovered the Dhamma that truly quenches *dukkha*, which he in turn shared with anyone interested. His goal was to produce a complete set of references for present and future research and practice. His approach was always scientific, straightforward, and practical.

Although his formal education was limited to seven years, plus some beginning Pali studies, he has been given eight honorary doctorates by Thai universities. Numerous doctoral theses have been written about his work. His books, both written and transcribed from talks, fill a room at the National Library and influence all serious Thai Buddhists.

Progressive elements in Thai society, especially the young, have been inspired by his wide-ranging thought, teaching, and selfless example. Since the 1960s, activists and thinkers in such areas as education, social welfare, and rural development have drawn upon his teaching, advice, and friendship. His work has helped inspire a new generation of socially concerned monks.

Since the founding of Suan Mokkh, he studied all schools of Buddhism and all the major religious traditions. This interest was practical rather than scholarly. He sought to unite all genuinely religious people, meaning those working to overcome selfishness, in order to work together for world peace. This broadmindedness won him friends and students from around the world, including Christians, Muslims, Hindus, and Sikhs.

In the last few years of his life, Buddhadāsa established an International Dhamma Hermitage. Here courses for introducing foreigners to the correct understanding of Buddhist principles and practice are held in English at the beginning of every month. Retreats in Thai are also organized. Further, he hoped that meetings would be organized for Buddhists from around the world to identify and agree upon the "Heart of Buddhism." Third, he wanted to bring together all the religions to cooperate in helping humanity.

He also established some new projects for carrying on the work of serving the Lord Buddha and humanity. One is Suan Atammayatārāma, a small training center for foreign monks in a quiet grove near the retreat center. The guidelines he laid down aim to develop "Dhamma Missionaries" who are well versed in the Buddha's teaching, have solid experience of *vipassanā*, and can adapt Buddha-Dhamma to the problems of the modern world.

A sister project is called Dhamma Mātā (Dhamma Mothers). Society is suffering from the lack of women spiritual teachers; they exist but are not given adequate recognition. Dhamma Mātā is for raising the status of women by providing better opportunities and support in Buddhist monastic life and meditation practice. The hope is that we will have more women who can "give birth to others through Dhamma."

Ajahn Buddhadāsa died at Suan Mokkh on July 8, 1993. The work of Suan Mokkh continues to this day as before, according to the law of nature.

THE TRANSLATOR, Dhammavicayo, was born in England in 1958. He was ordained as a monk in 1980, and now resides in Northeast Thailand.

THE EDITOR, Santikaro Bhikkhu, was born in Chicago and came to Thailand with the Peace Corps in 1980. Ordained in 1985, he came to Suan Mokkh in order to study with Buddhadāsa Bhikkhu. No longer a monk, he now teaches at Liberation Park in rural Wisconsin.

Other Books by the Author

Mindfulness with Breathing: A Manual for Serious Beginners
ISBN 978-0-86171-111-6 | 160 pages
Using a straight-forward style of presentation, Buddhadāsa Bhikkhu provides all you need to know to become free of stress and worry through the "simple and beautiful act of sitting quietly, alive to the breathing," as taught by Buddha in his Ānāpānasati Sutta.

Under the Bodhi Tree: Buddha's Original Vision of Dependent Co-arising
ISBN 978-1-61429-219-7 | 224 pages
Inquiry into dependent co-arising partners with exploration of voidness to foster the insights that free us from clinging to "me" and "mine." This translation captures Ajahn Buddhadāsa's understanding of how suffering is created and how it quenches.

Many of Buddhadsa's teachings are freely available at www.suanmokkh .org/archive/. Others of his most popular works are listed here:

Handbook for Mankind
Theravāda Buddhist religious experience in modern terms one need not be afraid to think about. An overview of the whole of Buddha-Dhamma: basic concerns, morality, meditation, insight, and the fruits of practice.

145

Keys to Natural Truth
Five talks dealing with fundamental issues of Dhamma understanding and practice. Offers key perspectives with which to sort out the essential teachings from cultural admixtures.

Buddha-Dhamma for University Students
Direct, clear replies to common questions asked by thinking people when they seriously examine Buddhism. Issues covered include emptiness, *karma*, rebirth, suffering, lay practice, the enlightened being, and *nibbāna*.

Practical Dependent Origination
A fresh look at the crucial teaching of dependent origination. Reasons why the traditional interpretations are unlikely to be the Buddha's intention. How to understand and practice dependent origination today, for liberation in this life.

Dhammic Socialism
Controversial essays exploring what a Dhamma-based society and economy might be like. Politics and economics viewed from the perspective of nonattachment.

Me and Mine
Collection of revised and condensed translations covering the broadest spectrum of Ajahn Buddhadāsa's teaching so far available in English.

Christianity and Buddhism
A Buddhist scholar and meditation master looks for practical nourishment in the Bible. In doing so, he challenges both Christian and Buddhist dogmatism.

About Wisdom Publications

Wisdom Publications is the leading publisher of classic and contemporary Buddhist books and practical works on mindfulness. To learn more about us or to explore our other books, please visit our website at wisdomexperience.org or contact us at the address below.

Wisdom Publications
199 Elm Street
Somerville, MA 02144 USA

We are a 501(c)(3) organization, and donations in support of our mission are tax deductible.

Wisdom Publications is affiliated with the Foundation for the Preservation of the Mahayana Tradition (FPMT).